Captains of Leadership

BISPUBLISHERS

Captains of Leadership

Build your Facilitative Confidence

Alwin Put

Copyright © 2021 Alwin Put and BIS Publishers

BIS Publishers
Borneostraat 80-A
1094 CP Amsterdam
The Netherlands
+31 (0)20 515 02 30
bis@bispublishers.com
www.bispublishers.com
www.captainsofleadership.com

ISBN 978 90 6369 619 1

Cover and inside design, illustrations: Tine van Wel,
tinevanwel.nl
Final editing: Gilleske Kreijns, bureautxt.nl

For my dad, you are the best listener a son could ever wish for.

In loving memory of my mother-in-law, Hilda Smeets.
With every butterfly passing by, we think about you.
You will always be in our hearts.

Prologue   9

Introduction   13

Part 1: The ship is sailing

1. Everything is connected   21
2. It really is a ship   31
3. Facilitation for coherence   39
4. Open Focus   45
Conclusion Part 1   53

Part 2: Get on board

5. The Moment   59
6. Guide   67
7. Conduct   97
8. Catalyse   135
Closure   161

Part 3: Sail into the sunset

9. Prepare for success   165
10. Manage your state   173

Captain-to-captain   197

Glossary   202
Acknowledgement   206

Prologue

Dad ... so what is it exactly that you do?

ON A WINTERY THURSDAY evening, right after having dinner with my family, I was staring at a big wall full of sticky notes. My office was now a guest bedroom turned into a war room, with a wall full of strategies and thoughts. A shelve in the closet, at eye height, has become the 'broadcasting space' to deliver all my online courses and workshops. We are in the middle of COVID times, and this room has become the center of my professional existence. No wonder the question about what I do comes up in both my sons' minds. They are obviously wondering what the hell I am doing to this room in our house. And where will grandma sleep when she stays over? Obviously, we didn't have any guests staying over for a long time. And I'm secretly hoping I do not have to take down my sticky wall-art any time soon.

One by one, my family enters my space, which I have been decorating during the hours of working alone at home. First, my oldest son enters with an elated expression on his face, seemingly thinking his dad is up to something big. Then, my other son enters the room, the one with the curly hair who loves to loudly express his feelings. He immediately shouts out loud: 'Wow dad! Is *that* what you do for work?' My wife is the last one to enter and says with a grin: 'You have clearly started working on your book.' My sons both look at me with big blue and green eyes and they ask me whether I am really writing a book. They're 9 and 7 years old, and they probably have their Marvel heroes and Harry Potter in the back of their minds when asking me. I cannot really believe it myself, and I sometimes still wonder why I embarked on this rollercoaster journey of writing a book. With the most confident voice I am able to produce at that moment, I confirm with a hopefully impressive 'yes', followed by a feeling of blind butterflies bumping into the inside of my stomach.

I have never written a book, but I have read quite a few great ones. All the respect I have for these amazingly smart and witty authors now gives me a feeling of humility. Am I capable of writing anything meaningful? I guess one brave day not too long ago, someone who seems to be me decided I could write something people want to read. The next fretful 'me' then started writing random bits and pieces of knowledge on sticky notes in an attempt to hopefully end up with some kind of common thread.

My oldest son, obviously impressed with my very confident 'yes', pops the question of which I am sure every parent thinks: 'How am I going to explain this without losing their interest after the first five words?' He asks me what it is exactly that I do for work. From the corner of my eye, I see the grin on my wife's face widening, probably enjoying this moment. I am sure she is curious as to how I will explain this while keeping our boys interested. She knows how I always eagerly try to live up to the image of being the most entertaining and fascinating dad-hero.

Usually, my sons stop listening to my explanations after the first couple of sentences. My oldest son already senses how much I am trying, so he will just pretend to listen as he keeps watching me, while his mind is clearly deviating towards other much more relevant things, like what our dog might be doing. Our youngest one usually just brutally walks away when I start explaining my philosophies. And I do love his honesty. So now, with a slight hesitation and with the hope that I will be able to amaze them, I start explaining that my job is about helping people in organizations to come up with new and better solutions. He looks at me and says: 'No, but what is the book about?', still probably with an exciting vision of Chris Hemsworth in his mind, holding his powerful hammer in the air, shooting out thunder and lightning across the sky.

I continue with: 'What if you would build something. Who would you build it with?' He replies: 'Well, dad, I would probably build it with my friends Tim, Peter, Ben and Bob.' My youngest one agrees with some serious affirmative nodding. 'And why would you want to build something with them?', 'Because I always do things with them, they are my friends, I know what they can do.' He is now looking at me as if he is wondering how long this explanation is going to take. 'Right! And let's say you are building a boat. And you have already decided to build it with your friends because each of them has something to contribute. Maybe Tim is tall and strong and can carry heavy things. Peter might know his way with the tools, while Ben is good at drawing plans, and Bob knows a thing or two about water.' 'Yeah, dad, and I'm really good at telling jokes when we're working together!' His face lights up. Now, I am sure I am off to a good start. My youngest one asks: 'How fast is this boat? I know he is double-checking whether this story is really worth his time. I immediately reply: 'This boat is going to be faster than lightning, because you can help to build it too.' 'Boom!', to use their word when you've done something amazing. Now I have got their full attention. They're staring at me, waiting for me to continue explaining.

I ask them: 'How would you now start building this boat?' My oldest son answers: 'We would decide what each of us will do, and … then we'll just go about doing what we agreed upon.' Then I ask him: 'Should there be any order to things? Should Tim first gather some heavy wooden planks, before Peter takes out his tools? Or should Ben first draw a plan of the boat? The youngest one replies loudly: 'Ben should first draw the boat!' My oldest son agrees: there should be an order of things for it to work well. He says: 'I will be the captain, I'll make sure everyone can do their best to build the boat together.' I ask him: 'Will you be telling jokes all the time then?' He thinks about it for a second, and part of him wants to say 'yes, of course', but the other part thinks about not being taken seriously or maybe distracting his friends and ending up with a sinking bunch of wooden planks. He replies: 'I think when I'm making sure everyone sticks to the plan, and I'm making it easy for them to do their thing, I would probably hold off on the jokes a bit. Just to make sure they pay attention to what they're doing.' Astonished by his sense of responsibility, I ask: 'And would it be best if you were always the captain?'

Again, he needs some time to ponder this question. Of course, he thinks that he should probably be the captain forever, but on the other hand he realizes it is not really only his boat, it is *their* boat. And what about all the adventures on the boat during which he might just want to be something else, like maybe the crew entertainer. And so he replies: 'Dad, I think I might be captain until the boat is finished. My friends are probably really good at building it, and I want to make sure I keep an eye on them, so we end up with a really nice boat. I would actually call it a ship, honestly. But then, when we go on adventures, I'm thinking I might be something else than the captain. Maybe I want to be a 'treasure-map-reader' or I might want to tell jokes and be funny.'

Now I ask them: 'Wouldn't that mean you're all captains on your ship? And depending on which adventure you're sailing towards, and how everyone wants to be part of that adventure, the right person will pick up the captain's hat to help make it the best adventure ever?' They look at me with wonderment. I am expecting cheers and some more serious nodding. Unimpressed, my oldest son says: 'Well, yeah, that's how we always play together. Everyone gets their chance to be the boss or the bad guy, or even the captain.' 'OK', I reply, 'that's what I teach adults, and that's what I'm writing about in the book. It's about how they can make better boats and have greater adventures when everyone gets to be the captain whenever it makes sense.'

My youngest son asks: 'Are you writing a book about boats then?' And I tell him: 'No, not really, that was just an example. It is more about how it is important to have good "captains" if you want people to work well together.' He looks at me confused, gets up and walks away to do something more fun. This story was clearly not about a lightning-fast boat. My oldest son tells me: 'Hey dad, that's kind of cool, it's good that you're writing this book.' And suddenly, I have a vision of someone standing on a hill with a hammer shooting out thunder and lightning, and it is not Chris Hemsworth, … it is me. In big bold letters, right above my hammer, it says 'Captains of Leadership'. And so the title of this book was born.

Introduction

This book is called *Captains of Leadership* because I believe there should be a form of leadership that we can all apply whenever necessary. Leadership is about getting the best out of people, and you should not need a title, promotion or status to do this. You just need to know how and when to make the most impact. Therefore, we all own the concept of leadership.

We are all Captains of Leadership. The reason I refer to captains is because the most inspiring characters to me, whether fictive or real, have been captains. What they all have in common is that they stand amongst their team members, they know their people, they aim to bring out the best in them. You can find them in sports, in movies, in space, …

Captains of Leadership is a book I have been wanting to write for a long time. I have met so many different people when teaching facilitation courses. And although it should be me providing them with all kinds of insights, I learn so much more from the participants when I observe them. What I have learned over the years is that people are generally quite nervous about being the facilitator. It obviously depends on the situation, whether they know the participants in their facilitation assignment, or how ambitiously high the goals are set. But in any situation, the facilitator will feel some form of vulnerability when taking on the responsibility to lead a team to the best outcomes of their collaboration.

SOME THINK THAT FACILITATION is a basic skill that almost everyone can learn. Other people describe the ability to facilitate as a gift, a talent that you are born with. I have heard people say that it is very hard to master and takes a lot of practice. Other people see it as just another course to follow and a skill to carry under their belt. I have seen course participants with a lot of experience in facilitation struggling with delivering just half an hour of smooth facilitation. Others who did not have a lot of experience immediately delivered a perfectly facilitated moment. From my experience, the key characteristic of great facilitators is not necessarily talent or experience. It is self-awareness. Self-awareness is not something

The key characteristic of great facilitators is not necessarily talent or experience. It is self-awareness.

you are born with, and you cannot learn it in a course. Good facilitators are just very conscious of themselves and other people.

There is one thing that most of the facilitators – and aspiring facilitators – I come across have in common. Facilitation comes with a certain level of vulnerability. All of them have memories of challenging and awkward situations in their professional lives. When at the start of a facilitation course I ask the participants about their expectations, more than half of them answer that they want to build their confidence as a facilitator. And these are all people who already have experience with facilitation. There are probably so many more amazing facilitators out there who lack the confidence to step up and lead the meeting or session. I believe it really matters that they find the confidence to do so. Everyone can make a huge difference by facilitating other people.

In this book I mostly refer to moments when a group of people have a moment of sharing thoughts and opinions to build on each other's perspective with the intention to arrive at certain agreement to take action. I refer to all those moments as co-creation, in the broadest sense of the word. If you sit together to discuss something in order to afterwards act upon it, I like to call it co-creation. It covers a broad spectrum of types of meetings and workshops. It can be your weekly team catch-up, an innovation workshop or a yearly sales meeting. It always comes down to sharing time together to create a better understanding of reality, and to lay the foundation for building a better reality in the smallest or most ambitious way.

I have read about influential and amazing people like Elon Musk and Jeff Bezos suggesting meetings should be shorter or even avoided completely. Here, I want to add another option. Maybe it would make a difference if we had excellent facilitators available to make a meeting count. What if facilitation was not just about creating an agenda and leading a group of people through it? What if facilitators were self-aware, empathic people with a knack for blending egos into a highly performing collective? Would it not make sense to sometimes even prolong a meeting because of the amazing stuff coming out?

My aim is for you to come to a new understanding of the impact you can have as a facilitator. And how important it is for you to pick up that role when you see the need. I will make the case that facilitation is the purest form of leadership. After explaining the significance of being a facilitator, I will share the most important things you need to know how to become excellent at it. And when you are ready to kick ass, I would like to invite you to pass on this book to the next person, so we can multiply and build an army of facilitators.

This world can be better if we have more people with the guts to step up to facilitate when they feel it really matters. I also believe there are enough books about 'Creative confidence'. So, here is one about 'Facilitative confidence'. I would consider it an enormous achievement if this book were to provide a language for things unsaid. If it would help us to discuss the facilitator's vulnerability amongst each other. If it would enable us to share awkward or discouraging facilitation experiences and help us to learn from each other and support each other to build our facilitative confidence together.

A THREE-PART, DIVERGENT BOOK

The first part of this book will be about the big 'why'. It will explain that it is worth all the effort to develop yourself as a facilitator. You will read about why facilitation is now more important than ever. You will also learn how facilitation is all about leadership, and what is really the essence of facilitation. This part will set the scene for Part 2 and Part 3.

In the second part of this book, you will learn about 'how' to facilitate. You will be introduced to the holy trinity of facilitation: Guiding, Conducting and Catalysing.

These three different aspects are explained separately, but they actually work in synergy when applied. This provides you with a basic structure to develop yourself as facilitator. It can serve as a framework helping you to identify your strengths and your areas of development.

The things I teach you in Part 2 are applicable immediately. So, start experimenting with every opportunity you come across to make this holy trinity your own. All the elements you will learn about here are written from personal experience. It has been tried, tested and ready for you to test and shape even further. The techniques are initially described for excellent facilitation of any type of gathering in your professional life, but it might even be interesting to test out some of them in your personal life.

As a facilitator, you are often the person in the room with the broadest open view on the challenge at hand. You are the observer. You are not participating, allowing you to be fully present. As you are leaning into the moment, you have the privilege to notice possibilities which participants might not see immediately. Helping them to gain new insights of new possible realities, helping them to come up with these themselves, often takes quite some energy and focus. Part 3 is about how you get into the right frame of mind and keep your energy level high. It explains how you can get to the best 'captaineering': getting the best out of your crew.

As you read this book, you will notice that there is little to no reference to other work or research. My intention is to make the content as practical as possible, but also as open as possible. I do not believe there is only one truth or only one way of doing things. This book will not provide you with a one-size-fits-all solution for all your workshops, nor will it make any definitive conclusions or does it try to be an authority on facilitation. This book will provide you with all kinds of real-life experiences and perspectives coming from facilitators who have gone through years of sessions with people from all over the world, in all kinds of settings. This book is written to inspire you and to entice you to start experimenting: it is intended to help you build your facilitative confidence.

In order to grow, you need to build your own stories and your own experiences. That is why this is a non-convergent book. It will not converge into any theoretical statements or models. You will not find any graphs, quadrants or statistics. The content is not built on quantitative data, but rather on qualitative insights. You are free to diverge even further, to broaden any concepts you read about. Feel free to rename techniques and build your own glossary.

In order to grow, you need to build your own stories and your own experiences.

I strongly believe it is necessary for us to break away from our conventional way of thinking about leadership and facilitation. The last thing this book should do is to create new fixed beliefs about both. Rather, it should open up possibilities and nurture connection between people. Feel free to agree to disagree with any interpretations I share from my own experiences. The only thing I expect from you as a reader is to consider facilitation if you have not done so before.

The word 'facilitation' already has so many inaccurate associations to so many people. With this book, I would like to redefine facilitation as a form of leadership. Moreover, a form of leadership that the world really needs right now. A form of leadership that is evolving along with our evolving level of consciousness. An open form of leadership that is selfless and serving the growth of all people. Therefore, I will often refer to facilitation (or facilitative leadership) as being a captain, or 'captaineering'. Simply because I believe you deserve hero status if you take on the role of a facilitator. You deserve the status of captain. We all do if we take on the facilitative leadership role at moments when we believe we can serve a group of people by helping to get the best out of their synergy. At the end of this book I will address you again, as captain to captain.

Now, batten down the hatches and catch the wind of change …

Twenty years from now you will be more disappointed by the things that you didn't do than by the ones you did do. So throw off the bowlines. Sail away from the safe harbor. Catch the trade winds in your sails. Explore! Dream! Discover! – **Mark Twain**

For more infromation about classes and workshops, go to www.captainsofleadership.com.

Part 1:
The ship is sailing

The wind and the waves are always on the side of the ablest navigator. – Edward Gibbon

1. Everything is connected

Early on in my career, I was convinced that I needed to come up with the best out-of-the box solutions, that it was necessary to become an expert in my field, and that I needed to climb the corporate ladder in order to be successful. All that changed when I discovered human-centered design and facilitative leadership. It really is the form of leadership we need to navigate this complex world of interrelated systems.

IT HAS BEEN MORE than twenty years since I first came across *The Experience Economy* by B. Joseph Pine II and James H. Gilmore. Research for the thesis I was writing about Mass Customization and E-commerce led me to this discovery. It made so much difference to me at the time. It shaped my plans for the future: I wanted to help companies build exceptional customer experiences, just like Gilmore and Pine described in their book.

Not long after, I co-founded a marketing agency called Xperienz. Our mission was to help small and mid-size companies to build lasting customer experiences. We were ready to conquer the world, standing on the shoulders of Pine and Gilmore. But after building some nice websites, creating brand identities and organizing corporate events for a handful of clients, we realized we were not going to make the expected dent in the universe.

I was so captivated by insights from the book, I could only see a world in need of compelling customer experiences. In my enthusiasm, I became blind to other perspectives.

For example, we had shop owners asking for simple give-away shopping bags with their logo on it. I suggested the most out-of-the-box shopping bag concepts to them. But they chose to buy their bags from the cheaper, 'more straightforward' supplier. In those early days I learned my first lesson about being biased and not understanding the real immediate needs. Sometimes, they just needed a straightforward solution. This is when I first started to discover my blind spots. But it took me a few more years to see the whole picture.

BIAS AND BLINDNESS

I used to be convinced that competitiveness was necessary to be successful. During my first years at the headquarters of Starwood Hotels

& Resorts, a renowned hospitality company, Six Sigma was a big thing. Earning your belts in Six Sigma was a great way to advance your career. It started with a yellow belt, and then you could climb up all the way to the master black belt. With a black belt you were fit to lead and manage projects. And this belt would also generate respect from peers. Six Sigma emphasized the operational perspective in collaboration. I would even say, it created an operational bias in problem-solving.

A few years into my career at headquarters, in the customer-facing camp of branding and marketing, customer journey mapping became a big thing, and so did everything relating to search engine optimization and social media strategy. Suddenly, everything seemed to be about storytelling and driving engagement. This resulted in entertaining discussions about key performance measurement and return on investment. Does a 'click', a 'like', a cheerful emoji or a good review put heads in beds? It probably does, but it is hard to make the direct link. Knowledge about Google Analytics and the ever-changing mechanics to drive visibility and engagement on social channels gave you stardom in our camp. Budgets were allocated towards digital campaigns and a lot of effort was made to give offline guest experiences a digital component. This focus emphasized the digital perspective in our internal collaboration. It created a digital bias, everything needed to feed into social engagement, or it had to have a digital component.

Across my career in corporate, I experienced a lot of tunnel vision discussions, fueled by the next big thing and strong one-sided beliefs. When people build up expertise, it becomes a great part of their perspective, and even of their identity. It becomes part of their world view. In a competitive environment, people defend their point of view as if it were the absolute truth. And yes, I did it too: often took a stand for certain new beliefs I acquired. I would defend them and try to bring my arguments as strong as possible when collaborating with other people. At the time, I was not aware of the polarizing effect it created.

Why do we develop blind spots and bias? Over the years I have become more aware of this polarizing effect that creates a bias and a blindness to other perspectives. I came to understand there are two simple reasons why my focus would narrow. The first one is the urge to control. With so many moving elements around me and me being unsure of how to become an acknowledged and significant part of the organization, taking a stand on certain viewpoints would give me a sense of control.

This urge to control is only half of the story. I would also act and think along the lines of competition. I like to refer to this as acting and thinking out of a sense of separation from others. As if we are not a collective and our priority is taking care of ourselves. This is the second reason why my focus would narrow: **acting and thinking from a sense of separation**.

I often felt the pressure to perform. I felt that my performance would be measured against that of others. I got caught up in a competition for the benefits and rewards to be gained. I aimed for the intrinsic rewards of being acknowledged as a talented and valued person. And I was seduced by the extrinsic motivational rewards: the bigger car, larger office with or without the 'door', the impressive title, the access to elite meetings behind closed doors. The types of benefits that are meant to be scarce and act as a 'carrot'. And still, many organizations today use individual extrinsic rewards to generate a pressurizing amount of competition. They fuel this feeling of separation, as if you need to fight and struggle to make something of yourself. As if it is essential to earn scarce benefits while competing with others.

MY MINDSET SHIFT

While reading books and articles about the next big thing in an effort to become an acknowledged expert in the domain of Marketing and Branding, I stumbled upon Design Thinking, aka human-centered design. A methodology which I was convinced I needed to master if I wanted to become the expert in building the best brand experiences. As I learned more and more about it, ironically, I became aware that wisdom is not about knowing facts and being the topic expert. Wisdom is about asking the right questions. This was a mindset shift for me. I got hooked on Design Thinking. The practice taught me how be open to other perspectives, to recognize my blind spots and replace control with serendipity.

Wisdom is not about knowing facts and being the topic expert. Wisdom is about asking the right questions.

25

Thankfully, the world is changing. We are now reaching a point where our awareness is collectively broadening to all perspectives. I notice companies are focusing on providing broad solutions, taking into account multiple stakeholders. Products are becoming hybrid, consisting of offline and online products and services. Local communities, natural resources and ecological footprint are on the strategic agenda and they influence consumers' buying decisions. We seem to be moving to a society where the value of organisations is not only measured by their financial performance but also their impact on society and natural resources.

Is our collective awareness evolving to understand and see the world as a set of interconnected ecosystems? Looking at the fast-paced developments in blockchain which allow peer-to-peer innovations; our lightning-speed exchange of perspectives and information on social; our renewed understanding of our human role to care for all living things; our raising concerns about the fragile balance in nature, I would say yes (it is a hopeful yes.) We have never been more connected than we are at this moment. And I strongly believe in the new generation of young leaders who are growing up in this connected world with many more social and ecological concerns than I had in my teenage years. I believe we are moving towards a collective worldview of interconnected ecosystems. We are evolving into a world of less separation, less control, and more co-creation.

We are evolving into a world of less separation, less control, and more co-creation.

How to understand systems. Any living creature impacted by others in a specific way makes up a system of specific interactions with its own context and rules. Multiple systems are linked to each other and they impact each other. In all directions, everything is clustered within cultures, structures, agreements, responsibilities, shapes and forms of interactions. They are interrelated, meaning any kind of network between entities is related to any other network. But you could also say systems are nested, meaning they exist within each other, like a Russian babushka doll. You can keep defining a broader and broader and broader context. Like the example of a family living in a village, within a region, within a province, within a country, within a continent, etc.

So, each time we refer to a system, we are actually referring to living entities that interact with each other in some way, according to certain habits, rules, policies, stated or unstated agreements. Often, there is some kind of value exchange; there is a reason for an interaction. All parties get something out of the interaction, even if it is not a desired output.

But a system is built on more than merely value transactions. It becomes more complicated when you also imagine all the invisible forces connecting and impacting the behaviour of entities in a system. Like the impact of gravity. Or dynamic influences like the changes in temperature and light brought on by different seasons. Or the acquisition of a start-up with a funky laid-back culture, to be embedded in a traditional banking organisation. Trying to imagine a world consisting of systems, from the smallest micro-level to a planet-wide macro-level, confronts us with a high level of complexity. Especially when you consider that these systems are all in flux. Any system you can think of will be different the next time you think about it.

How can we govern this complexity? I do not believe we should try to control the complex maze of interrelated and nested systems that build up our reality. It is just not possible. Especially when there is a high level of complexity involved. One obvious reason why we cannot control this complexity is because we are unable to comprehend the dynamics with our limited consciousness. So, we need to manage our urge to control. This can be done by applying the power of facilitation.

Let's start by looking at our more comprehensible organisational systems. Inspired by the openness of Design Thinking – and good facilitation – all stakeholders in the system could thrive, provided you can improve the quality of the interactions between them. Those interactions within an organisational system, where new future realities are conceived, are the moments that really matter. If we could uplift all those interactions with facilitation, it might uplift a complete organisational system in flux. With facilitation, you can build on the flux, build on the momentum of the system, to drive the change that benefits all people involved.

It requires an open mindset, empathy, and a co-creative attitude: the opposite of control and separation. It really needs a form of decentralised leadership, which I like to refer to as facilitative leadership. And every organisation should have an army of facilitators.

27

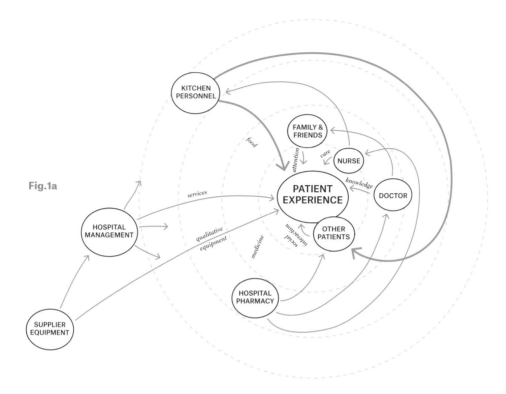

Fig.1a

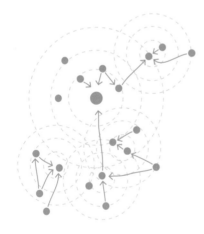

Fig.1b

Fig. 1a This is a simple rendition of the system influencing a patient experience. Multiple stakeholders influence this experience with a direct or indirect impact. The intensity of the relationship to the center is shown by the distance of the circles. The stakeholders often influence each other's opinions and behavior. The interaction between them and with the patient consist of all kinds of exchanges like services, care, expertise, budget, equipment, etc. If you change the behavior of one of the stakeholders, it will influence the behavior of all the other stakeholders. This is a static and simplified display of a system which in reality is much more complex.

Fig. 1b If you look beyond the patient experience, you will see that every stakeholder influences – and is influenced by – many more elements. At any given time, our experiences in life are impacted by a lot of people, and our thoughts and actions impact the experience of many other people, not even mentioning the non-human stakeholders. This figure shows the increase in complexity when adding circles of 'influence' around each stakeholder. The circles represent influences and relationships in other systems. This is still a static representation. All these influences and stakeholders within systems of interactions and relationships are continuously in flux.

STAKEHOLDER MAPPING

When I try to visualise the complexity of systems, I make use of a simple stakeholder mapping technique. It is as simple as it is genius to help you to better understand a system.

Step 1. Draw a circle in the middle of a blank page. Add anything you are focusing on to that circle. It could be a challenge, a person or a general topic.

Step 2. Draw another circle around this central circle. This distance represents the intensity of the relationship between any entities in this second circle and your focus point in the middle.

Step 3. Draw some more circles, each time expanding with equal distance from the previous circle. The distance from the circle to the centre keeps representing how closely related any entities in this circle might be to the focus point in the centre.

Step 4. You might have guessed: now add any related entities or stakeholders to the circles. The distance of the circle represents the intensity of the connection between the stakeholder and the centred focus point. It might be that the entity is heavily impacted by the challenge, or the entity influences the centred person to a large extent.

Step 5. Try to define the connection between the stakeholders and the center. Draw an arrow and write on the arrow any characteristics relevant to the relationship and interaction. For example, is it a transactional value exchange of some sort (monetary, expertise, service), or is it an experiential value exchange (attention, support, friendship)? There is no right or wrong here, it is just the description that makes most sense at this moment.

Step 6. Now see if there are any other arrows and descriptions needed in between stakeholders and add them. Result. You have a visual overview of an interpreted static snapshot within a system.

This practice can help you to prepare for any type of assignment. If you need to make a proposal as an Account Manager, you can add your buyer at the centre and add any influential stakeholders on the different rings, revealing in what way they influence the buying decision of the buyer. The buying decision can be influenced by the advice from procurement, or maybe it is the financial department, or an external consultant and topic expert.

If you need to go out and do some research, it could help to map your research topic at the centre, and map all involved stakeholders at different distances, describing their link to the topic of research. This visual overview enables you to decide in which order you would like to proceed and what kind of question you should ask whom.

Fig.1a shows you an example of a mapped-out static snapshot of a system. It is often called a Stakeholder Map. Remember I referred to interrelated and nested systems? Imagine you would consider each stakeholder on your map to be another centre. And again you can add circles around this stakeholder, as shown in **fig.1b**. You could repeat this process endlessly. It will show how any impact any stakeholder has on a centred stakeholder, also impacts the connection this centred stakeholder has on the initial centred topic or stakeholder.

Now this is a static representation of the connections, as if they were always activated. As we know, interactions are moments and each of them is unique. These interactions are like pulses, and the arrow representing the connection fades in and out. Each time an arrow or an interaction occurs between stakeholders, it generates an effect on the interactions between all the other connected stakeholders. This means that the interactions create ripple effects among the connected stakeholders and systems.

Just try to imagine for a couple of seconds how these millions of moments of interaction, within millions of interrelated systems, generate even more ripple effects across stakeholders. It makes you wonder whether we should just drop the idea of 'control' altogether? Instead, we need to consider the question of how to navigate this complexity.

I am sure only one captain will not be enough to navigate this universe. We should all be captains of leadership. But then what kind of leadership are we talking about here?

2. It really is a ship

We need to let go of the idea that leadership is an earned status. Facilitative leadership is not a privilege, it is a state of mind and a role anyone can assume when it matters.

I HAVE SPENT MANY years working in corporate environments, and it has taught me a lot about leadership. I have experienced many different kinds of interactions with people in leadership roles, while working in Communication Design, Marketing and Brand Management. On the flip side, I also experienced moments of truth when I was regarded as a leader.

Funnily, my memories of 'leaders' are not defined by the actions which they probably think were memorable and impactful. I am sure a lot of people in leadership positions think it is their keynote speech, their forward thinking and track record, their decisive decision-making, their perseverance or steadiness in difficult times – or maybe just their overwhelming presence that makes a lasting impression on everyone. Not at all. It was not the 'big' moments that made them big leaders. It was how they behaved in the 'smaller' moments interacting with the people that really needed their guidance.

LEADERSHIP IS ABOUT HOW YOU MAKE PEOPLE FEEL

Looking back, the moments when leadership made a difference in my life were defined by the depth of the connection that was made each time we shared a moment. Maybe during a one-to-one setting, but also in a team setting. Obviously, the depth of connection is more challenging in larger groups, but I have known leaders who were able to connect deeply with a larger group, and it did not happen during a polished one-way speech. It happened when things settled down and the leader had everyone lean into the moment.

It was not their amazing presence, rather it was their openness and vulnerability. From all the leaders I have experienced in my professional life, only a handful made a lasting impression. They all have one thing in common: really being present in the moment we shared, when the team – or I – needed guidance. They were not imposing their opinions and point of view. They did not feel that they needed to live up a leadership title or image. Their strength was their authentic and empathic attention that brought out all available perspectives, talents and expertise.

Civil rights activist and writer Maya Angelou once said: 'People will forget what you said, and what you did, but they will never forget how you made them feel.' The handful of impressive leaders I met did not try to be the smartest person in the room. They did not earn trust because they had all the answers. They earned trust because they were really there for you. As a result, everyone gravitated towards them. Everyone wanted a slice of their time and attention.

> *'People will forget what you said, and what you did, but they will never forget how you made them feel.'*
>
> – Maya Angelou

The essence of leadership is about understanding, honoring and enabling key moments of co-creation. True leaders understand the importance of that moment when people spend time and space together with a purpose, no matter how small or how big. And they know that this moment will not live up to its full potential if 'busy-ness' gets in the way.

THE IDEAL INTERPRETATION

Leadership should not be an earned status. While writing this book I got curious about how other people experienced leadership in their lives. To find out, I asked two questions to a diverse group of about fifteen people. All of them are working in different industries, either reporting to leaders or having several reporting lines as a leader. First, I asked them which definition of leadership they would expect most people to agree with. Secondly, I asked the group what the ideal interpretation of leadership should be in the future.

On the first question, across all responses, they agreed that leadership is about providing direction within an inspiring vision. Leaders need to know how to kickstart execution and bring out the best in everyone. They also need to know how to get everyone to find their role when building that inspiring future reality. But they also allow for some space to question and interpret the approach, connecting different talents and experts, and empowering and coaching them. A good leader is there to see the execution through till the end.

To the second question, some respondents replied similarly, explaining further the necessity to inspire and empower. Others gave me an extra perspective. They said that, ideally, there would be no need for a leader. People would be able to self-manage. If there were still leaders, there should be an expansion of responsibility on both sides. Meaning that leaders, on their part, should be responsible for the personal growth of their people, actively helping them to better themselves. They would lead with empathy.

SOME OTHER RESPONSES WERE:

'Leadership currently feels too much like a goal. A promotion to achieve or a higher bonus – even if it means walking all over other people.'

'Somehow, it feels like people perceive "leadership" as the mere equivalent of "a manager or leader who obtains (great) business results".'

In my ideal world, leadership should be perceived as a genuine skill that lives within each individual, that can be measured on scales like curiosity, charisma, trust, …, getting the best out of every individual.

We all seem to agree that leadership is about being inspirational, giving clear direction, empowerment, ensuring execution, taking on end responsibility and building bridges. And yes, these are important leadership characteristics. But when assigned leadership becomes earned status – a title and position that separates you from the rest instead of connecting you – the lack of connection can result in a lack of trust. If leaders lead by reinforcing their status as a leader, they only impose their personal vision, which often will not result in genuine motivation and commitment.

LEADERSHIP WITH A RELAXED MIND

The handful of leaders who have been imprinted in my memory did not need to be assigned a leadership role to lead. They were leading long before they were officially promoted to a leadership position. It is a natural, empathy-infused state. They are not even aware they are applying skills and qualities that are taught in emotional intelligence courses. They are just very aware of themselves, the moment and other people. True leaders can deal with challenging situations while their mind is relaxed.

This is the type of natural leadership that gets the best out of people. It is not controlling, nor driven by competition and it is completely non-judgmental. It creates the space for people to connect and co-create. Leadership is not necessarily a person, and certainly not an earned status nor a privilege. Rather, it is a mindset that can be applied by anyone. When you detach leadership from titles and positions, it becomes a moment when someone can guide a group of people to the best outcomes. This is facilitative leadership. It is a fluid form of leadership, available to anyone who wants to lead in the moment.

A fluid form of leadership does not replace or exclude installed leadership. The difference is that installed leadership carries responsibilities that are part of the assigned role while fluid facilitative leadership consists of moments, and it can be taken on by anyone despite title or role. For example, a team meeting is often led by the team lead. But it can be very refreshing to have someone else from the team to the facilitating. The agenda and goal can still be briefed by the team lead, but the pre-reads, the flow, and the actual facilitation can be done by anyone from the team – or even outside the team.

Usually, outside people are invited to provide new perspectives or content in a team meeting. What if an outside person is invited to guide the thought processes of the team? This might really lead to a different way of thinking and potentially different or even better output. But it can be very refreshing to have someone else from the team do the facilitation.

Leadership is not necessarily a person, it is a mindset which can be applied by anyone.

In this vast world of clustered, interrelated and nested systems, a fluid form of facilitative leadership can enable synergies that benefit all involved stakeholders. As it is fluid, it is decentralized and therefore has agility and flexibility. In other words, it is a form of leadership that has a

36

broad reach across an organizational system when multiple people are trained in facilitative leadership.

Let's sail beyond the notion of leadership being a person. We will build better boats and have better adventures when we are all captains on this leadership, wearing and sharing our captain's hat when necessary.

In the next chapter I will explain what it means to wear your captain's hat.

3. Facilitation for coherence

So, what does it take to be a captain of leadership? What does it mean to wear the captain's hat? It takes a leadership state of mind to bring people together and get the most out of their shared moments. You need to connect people with their hands, heads and hearts.

WHEN CONNECTING PEOPLE with their hands, you provide them with clarity and structure. For people to do things effectively together, they first need to understand the work that needs to be done. When you get people to do things together, they also need to start thinking together. Connecting people with their heads is about creating a comfortable space to share perspectives and be open to different opinions. Interpreting and concluding together is not something that always happens smoothly in a group of different types of personalities and experts. The glue of the connection is the heart. You connect people with their hearts by fostering the idea that their belief in the purpose will keep them together – even when things get rough.

A facilitator aims for full participation, full engagement and fosters belief.

COHERENCE IS A STATE OF RESONANCE

The overarching goal of connecting people with hands, heads and hearts is achieving coherence within teams of people. I intentionally use the word coherence instead of cohesion. Team cohesion can be defined as a state in which people in the team stick together and support each other, which is a great team characteristic. But here I am referring to a state of resonance, where people build on each other's ideas and understand each other's perspectives. Coherence is about merging people from a group of individuals – with individual qualities and values – into an individual group. This is the main goal of facilitation. Facilitators are an extension of leadership, ensuring team coherence during moments of co-creation.

Incoherence between people is usually the default state in competitive organizational environments, where people think and act from a sense of separation. But even when the organizational environment is inclusive and non-competitive, people are targeted by all kinds of stressors in their lives. They might have had a stressful journey getting to work, they might struggle with family issues, they might be worried about a presentation they have to give or about a supplier who fails to deliver. Everybody is dealing with stress, whether is it work-related or personal. Unfortunately, people who are stressed are unable to reach that state of coherence, that state of deep connection. As a facilitator, you need to shape that 'moment' so that people will feel comfortable to open up and let go of their stressors.

And when you share such a moment, it could make a lasting impression on all those involved, just like that handful of leaders I told you about. What if those moments happen multiple times on a daily basis, across the organization, across offices and continents? If facilitative leadership is applied across the board, generating coherence between people, it will build a collaborative culture in an organization.

Why is achieving a state of team coherence so important? All the organizations I work with are in some stage of transformation. They are transforming their business digitally, restructuring to a more agile approach, streamlining operations to become lean and cost-efficient. Their aim is to become more innovative and increase or maintain their relevance in fast-changing markets. But people in an organization can only create new solutions from the unknown when they achieve coherence together. They need to be able to connect and empathize deeply, understanding each other's perspectives and building on them together. Without it, they will not be able to generate unconventional new solutions. If they think from separation, remain competitive, inconsiderate of each other's perspectives, they cannot co-create new realities for the organization. They will only play it safe and come up with conventional answers. They will stick to the known, because the unknown does not feel safe in a competitive environment. It does not feel safe. No matter which model or methodology is applied. Coherence is a key requirement for innovation. But it is not the natural state of a team when working together. It needs facilitative leadership.

GENERATING EMPATHY

Empathy is not only the ability to sense another person's emotions. It is the capability of living the other person's emotions and seeing things from their perspective without the bias of your own personality. It is a non-judgmental interpretation of how the other person experiences the world. When you can resonate with other people's thoughts and opinions, when you connect deeply to sense their world, there is a level of coherence between you and them. I have heard a neuroscientist calling it 'synchronization of the brain wavelength' between people. It has been shown through hyperscanning, where several people are interacting while their brains are simultaneously scanned, each in a separate MRI scanner. When people collaborate and emphatize, their brain start to resonate at the same wavelength.

When you connect deeply, there is a level of coherence between you and them.

An important consequence of coherence in a team is the ability to generate collective empathy. Highly empathic teams in coherence will not only generate disruptive solutions: they will also be targeting real needs with those disruptive solutions. The solutions will be human-centered. This makes a world of difference. Disruption and innovation can never be goals in themselves, you need to factor in empathy to actually make a positive impact on the world.

Too often, people struggle with letting go of their own perspective, let alone letting go of their personality, their beliefs, their way of interpreting the world. In everything we do, we usually strive to become good at it: we want to become experts. Whatever knowledge and skills we have built up, we tend to identify with. It renders meaning to who we are and why we exist. It also creates a frame of reference, a filter through which we interpret all the information that enters our brain. We like the feeling of having some kind of grip on what happens around us. Loosening this grip feels like giving way to uncertainty and insecurity, letting go of your own point of view.

Generally, when people enter a gathering, a meeting, a 'moment' of co-creation, they do not naturally step into the room with an open mind. It requires facilitative leadership to create a safe space for people to deeply connect. It also requires facilitative leadership to generate coherence amongst the team, enabling them to have a collective empathic understanding of any topic on the table. And it also takes facilitative leadership to help a team forward in making sensible decisions based on shared insights. A facilitator holds the space for everyone to achieve trust and appreciation towards each other, towards the shared moment and towards the facilitator.

So, what does it mean to wear the captain's hat? It means being able to facilitate for coherence and empathy. In other words: as a facilitator, you need to make sure the participants have an open focus.

In the next chapter I will tell you all about open focus and its opposite: narrow focus.

4. Open Focus

Coherence in co-creation creates better outcomes. It requires an open focus from everyone. Let me explain why this focus is so important.

WE ALL HAVE EXPERIENCES that can stir up feelings of uncertainty, fear, anger, frustration, disappointment, annoyance, loneliness, emptiness, inadequacy, guilt, and so on. I refer to these kind of emotions as 'demotions', because they can make you feel demotivated or depleted. Experiencing these demotions, it affects your body and your thinking. Your heart rate goes up and your breath becomes shallower. A voice in your head starts making up all kinds of stories to underpin the demotions, possibly even amplifying them. Your attention becomes focused on all the things that makes you feel this way. Your focus narrows to all the things that have not gone the way you wanted them to. And you start blaming elements from your outer environment. You blame other people, situations, time or even your body. You might not consider yourself beautiful enough, not healthy enough, not strong enough. When you get stuck in this narrow mindset, it can be hard to shift your attention to what other people might feel, to see the situation from a different perspective without judgment. You can get caught up in this narrow-minded thinking when you feel hurt or threatened.

This state is often called 'survival mode', but I like to refer to it as a 'narrow focus'. It is a built-in mechanism that helps us to survive when we feel threatened. Back when we lived more dangerous lives – when we lived as hunter-gatherers – this mechanism was very useful, for instance when we came across a saber-toothed tiger that was ready to attack us. When survival mode kicks in, your focus becomes narrow so you can use all our energy to fight or run. Your body starts producing stress hormones like adrenaline and cortisol to prepare your body to do everything necessary to survive. All energy is directed to your vital organs, which has a dampening effect on several other systems in your body, like the digestive system and the immune system.

This reaction, originally developed by evolution to save our lives, is triggered in our bodies even when we just feel threatened by our colleague or when someone in traffic cuts us off. The threats in our lifetime are more subtle than defending ourselves against wild animals. That is why I prefer to call it narrow focus instead of survival mode, we're not actually fighting or fleeing multiple times a day.

So, while the situations are different (sabre-toothed tiger vs. intimidating colleague), the physiological process is exactly the same. If you would do a brain scan when you are experiencing demotions, the activity in your brain will look more disorganised. An EEG to test the electrical activity in your brain would register high-frequency brainwaves called beta brainwaves. They range between 12.5 and 30 cycles per second. The sympathetic nervous system is activated, increasing heart rate and blood flow to the muscles, which happens in concert with the hormonal responses.

When you feel demotions that narrow your focus, you are limiting your perspective to only the things you know from experience.

When you feel demotions that narrow your focus, your perspective becomes limited to only the things you know from experience, and your attention is focused on the causes in your outer environment. Being in high beta means you are seeing the world from your ego, a one-sided perspective. In this state, it is almost impossible to empathize with other perspectives. In this state, you are stuck in the known, you just do not have the 'headspace' to come up with totally new associations. In other words, your thinking is predominantly analytical, and you have little access to broad associations made in your subconscious.

We are all triggered in our own unique way: the way we are triggered into a narrow focus is different for each person. It depends on our upbringing, intense emotional experiences in our lives, our age, our culture, our beliefs, …, a multitude of variables that build our worldview.

SUPERMARKET STRESS

For example, I struggle with impatience. When traffic is busy, or when I have to wait in line at the supermarket, I get nervous. It even happens

48

when I am planning a holiday or an interesting project. I have a hard time waiting for all the pieces to fall together and have the experience or 'do' things. Sometimes I notice similarities with my dad, and sometimes I notice similarities with my oldest son. I am guessing we are passing on some karma here.

When I know from memory that it will probably be busy at the supermarket, it will stir up certain programmed demotions, like restlessness, agitation and annoyance. These demotions appear before I have reached the parking lot, before the actual shopping experience. When I arrive, I notice all the cars and the fact that 'again' there is only parking space far away from the entrance. When I see that there are only a couple of trolleys left, I imagine the scene of trolleys bumping into each other in the cramped vegetable aisle. And while I pick up the final item on my grocery list – before finding my way to the registers – I can already feel the stress of choosing the right line.

And before all of that, when my wife asks me to go to the supermarket, my first thought is 'Oh, what day is it today?'. And if it is Saturday, nightmarish mental pictures of supermarket hell fill my head before I even get into my car. The demotions trigger my stress hormones, narrowing my perspective to only one thing: making sure I get out quickly and alive. I might even react inconsiderate to fellow shoppers, because Mr. Empathy is currently on a break, he's replaced by Mr. Ego.

Now imagine you had an intense emotional experience at work. You have been disappointed by management a couple of times. After all the work you have done, they still do not acknowledge or reward you. You feel insignificant or, worst case, invisible. Or maybe you have a hard time working with a certain colleague. Since you have been assigned to the same team, you have been arguing a lot. It seems impossible to compromise or find a common ground with this person. Experiences like this feed into your programming. Next time, you might expect to be disappointed by management even before they made any decision. Or maybe your start to feel agitated at the mere thought of the meeting with that colleague later in the day. An organizational environment is full of stressors. It is the place where you identify with your role and where you achieve successes while dealing with all sorts of challenges.

An organizational environment is full of stressors.

Your workplace is basically full of saber-toothed tigers that trigger your survival mode.

When people step into a meeting, expected to be open towards each other's opinions, they often just came from a tough phone call with a client, responding to agitating emails running behind on their schedule, disagreeing with their manager, etc. They come in with an activated survival mode. From their narrow focus, they see the world from an ego perspective. Especially in an intense organizational environment, and even more so if the environment is competitive, nurturing a culture of separation. You cannot avoid potential stressors. Because you have been programmed by your past experiences and related emotions, and these potential stressors can arise anywhere, at any time. But that does not mean the mechanism should always be triggered.

OPEN FOCUS: RESIDING IN THE PRESENT MOMENT

An open focus is the opposite of a narrow focus. Open focus means you are in a relaxed state of mind. I have asked hundreds of people in my courses when they get their best ideas. I get the same answers over and over again. 'When I'm in the shower.' 'When I'm waking up.' 'When I'm walking the dog.' 'When I'm driving my car.' 'When I'm fishing.' Ironically, they never tell me: 'When I'm sitting in a meeting room with my colleagues for a two-hour brainstorm.' An open focus is there when you are able to let go, when no urgent problem, issue or threat hijacks your attention. When you are not worrying about the past or the future, but when your attention fully resides in the present moment. In that state, your thinking becomes less analytical because there is no need to counter an imminent threat or problem. Instead, you now have the headspace for random associations to pop from your subconscious into your consciousness.

With a relaxed mind, an open focus, your brain activity is more organized. When you would use an EEG in this state, it would register lower frequency brainwaves, also called low beta and alpha brainwaves. Alpha is the range between 9 to 14 cycles per second, and typically called the 'creative state'. It is the state you are in when you are resting after completing a task. During a relaxed state of mind, the parasympathetic nervous system is activated, lowering heart rate and slowing breathing, providing more energy for systems like the digestive system. It basically is the opposite of the sympathetic nervous system, and it undoes the stress reactions in the body. If you see sympathetic nervous system as the accelerator, the parasympathetic system is the brake. People become more creative and they can better deal with complex problem solving when the parasympathetic nervous system is activated.

BECOMING SELF-AWARE

How can we manage an open focus? It works best when you are aware and accept that you will be challenged in life. When you feel demotions and notice your thoughts are reinforcing them, you still have a choice. If you pay attention to your breathing, you can activate your parasympathetic nervous system and increase alpha brain waves. It is important to understand that the key requirement is self-awareness. Being able to observe your feelings and thoughts, while not identifying with these feelings and thoughts, provides headspace to broaden your perspective and see things beyond your one-sided viewpoint. By doing so, you can transform the demotions into elevated emotions like gratitude, appreciation, fascination, etc. This will tell your body there is no threat, it is safe to rest and digest. It is not easy to learn how to avoid falling victim to your programming and not getting stuck in fixed beliefs. but it is definitely possible to learn how to freely observe yourself – your patterns – and choose your response to triggers. In Part 3, I will explain ways to practically manage your open focus.

The key requirement to managing an open focus is self-awareness.

So how this does work? How do I observe myself in order to maintain an open focus? In the supermarket case, I can shift my perspective away from the crowdedness and towards imagining how everyone is probably stressed at the supermarket on a Saturday. I can think about how it is not easy for all staff to cater to everyone's needs when most of the people are grumpy. I ask myself whether I really want to be one of those grumpy people. I observe myself as I start to feel anxious driving up the parking lot, and I realize how these thoughts are random and might be easily exchanged with different thoughts. I could even think about how happy I will make my family and friends with the amazing BBQ for which I am buying groceries. Observing my thoughts and feelings allows me to shift perspective and change my emotions to avoid stress responses and a narrow focus.

How can we manage the open focus of our team? Managing your own state is one thing, managing the focus of a group is yet another. As a facilitator, you need to promote an open focus amongst your participants. That is the way to generate coherence. Without an open focus, they will have a hard time deeply connecting and empathizing. They will not reach the level of understanding necessary to co-create novel solutions.

To make your team coherent, they should not feel threatened in any way. That is why a safe space is so important. When you create a space for co-creation, as a facilitator, you are designing a moment where everyone can have a relaxed mind and easily take into account different perspectives, with access to the broad new associations they make in their subconscious.

A non-threatening moment of co-creation allows for deep listening, synchronizing brains. When everyone is in the moment, not only the facilitator is holding space, everyone is holding space for each other. Holding space for others to fully express themselves will lead to the best interpretations and outcomes. This means deferring from any judgment and allowing for every aspect to be absorbed by your consciousness: the words, the tone, the expression, the body language, the overall moment. Clearly, participants are unable to do this when egos are cluttering the space with loud one-sided views.

The beautiful thing about listening with an open focus is that you do not even have to write anything down. Your memory will be performing optimally, and you will remember every aspect of the conversation vividly. If you are stressed, bothered or concerned, you will miss half of the things that are said, you will not pick up any details. The only thing you will probably pick up is the information that confirms your existing point of view.

To get coherence going within your team members, you need to build trust, direct their attention and energy and strengthen their belief in the cause. These are the foundations of a safe space and successful co-creation. In Part 2, I will show you how you can achieve this.

Conclusion Part 1

Captains of Coherence

EVERYTHING WE THINK and do has an impact on others. Everything is connected. With our growing awareness of systems – and how they are all interconnected – there is a growing sense of responsibility. Facilitation can uplift the interactions within a system, generating better outcomes for all stakeholders.

Facilitation is the type of natural leadership that brings out the best out in people. Leadership that is not controlling, not driven by competition and non-judgmental. It is the type of leadership that creates the space for people to connect and co-create. This kind of facilitative leadership is not a person, not an earned status nor a privilege, it is a mindset that anyone can apply. Therefore, it can be fluid and decentralized. It is an agile and flexible extension of installed leadership, that can have a broad reach across an organizational system.

Facilitative leadership is all about generating coherence between people. When people join a 'moment' of co-creation, they are not always ready to have an empathic understanding of what others will be sharing. It requires facilitative leadership to create a safe space for people to deeply connect. Highly empathic teams in coherence will not only generate disruptive solutions: they will also be targeting real needs with those disruptive solutions. Solutions that are human-centered.

An open focus is essential to creating coherence. Facilitative leadership creates and holds the space for people to open up. needs to, because open focus is not the default state of people collaborating in organizations. We are confronted with stressors that narrow our focus all the time.

With all the pressure on innovation, customer and employee delight, the necessary organizational agility can only come from self-managing teams. The older mechanical organizational models with fixed roles and reporting lines and mainly extrinsic individual rewards have become too rigid. Fluidity, agility, intrinsic motivation to drive full commitment of everyone are necessary to stay relevant.

But self-management is a product of self-awareness. You cannot achieve self-managing teams by teaching people to perform individually or by teaching them that only a few at the top have real decision power. You cannot nurture self-awareness when you nurture a sense of separation at the same time. Self-awareness can be nurturedacross the board by developing and installing decentralized facilitative leadership. Facilitative leaders lead by example at each gathering they facilitate, at each moment of co-creation. They are change agents to evolve culture.

Building your facilitative confidence starts with understanding the importance of your efforts as a facilitative leader. In the next part of this book, I will explain how to apply facilitative leadership.
It is the practical part of the book built from all my experiences as a facilitator. Before you start reading.

Part 2, I would like to suggest you create your Captain's log. In this notebook you can write down your experiments and the results whenever you try out anything you have learned from this next part. As you read though each chapter, you will find suggestions to put theory into practice.

Your Captain's log will become one of the most important treasures in your quest to become the best facilitator possible. As we are becoming Captains of leadership, hopefully one day we can share our logs with each other.

It is time! Raise the anchor …

Part 2:
Get on board

I'm not afraid of storms, for I'm learning how to sail my ship.
– Louisa May Alcott

5. The Moment

A moment is never just a moment, it is what you make of it

I HAVE JUST WALKED into the apartment and I can sense a peaceful calmness in the living room. She is lying on her bed by the window. The sun is shining in a different way. As if it is trying to keep her warm and comfortable. I walk over to her to let her know I have arrived. She opens her eyes slightly and says 'hi' with a short but gentle smile.

It is only us, just six of us, her closest family. We are soaking up every single minute, knowing these are the last ones in her presence. Every move and every sound, every teardrop slowly sliding down our cheeks, every carefully chosen word, nothing goes unnoticed. It feels like time is standing still, but we are still holding on to every minute with heightened senses. Every one of us is wondering what it will feel like when the moment arrives to let her go. She was such an important part of all our lives, it is hard to imagine what life will be like without her.

We all try to lighten the mood with some small talk. Everyone immediately digs into the chit-chat just to break the heavy silence. But the chit-chatting quickly turns into sharing memories about her, which now seem like another lifetime. We laugh about her typical stubbornness and uniquely strong personality. The way she carried her disease, just to make it easier on us, was absolutely astonishing. While sharing our memories, we all feel deeply connected in this surreal moment. A tender moment of love, fragility and pain, all at the same time. A moment that will be forever in our memories. One by one, we take the opportunity to sit close to her and whisper some comforting words. With the last life energy left in her body she is still able to crack some soft jokes to cheer us up. And when she does, the sun seems to be creating a halo around her. Our emotions are like a rollercoaster, for a moment it seems everything is calm and okay, and a minute later painful thoughts trigger panicky feelings. We all seem to be in sync, feeling what the others are feeling without expressing it.

The nurses walk in. Now it becomes real. We comfort each other by reminding ourselves that this is what she really wants. The pain is just too much. The nurses make all the preparations. Discussing some practicalities distracts us from what is to come. Until a bit later, right on cue, the doctor walks in. This is the start of the heartbreaking final act.

You are never prepared for such moments. They are so intense. And although time was standing still during those last hours, afterwards it felt like it flew by so quickly. When she was still with us, everyone was so present. The outside world did not exist. We were cherishing every last moment with her. When she left us, and this happened in a couple of seconds, suddenly reality kicked in. She was gone, it was over, the only thing left was a feeling of emptiness. We tried to escape from it by starting to organize all the next steps following this passing of a loved one.

This was such a pure moment and we fully experienced and shared it, until the last minute. When people share such an intense moment in time and space, there is much more than the eye can see. There is a connection, an interaction beyond words or body language. You can sense each other's feelings. In this moment, there was no room for judgment or friction. There were no egos, only loving presence. In such a moment, everyone becomes part of it. You blend into a collective experience, you resonate with each other, there is coherence.

CREATING THE MOMENT

These kinds of moments create bonds and are imprinted in your memory. In this special situation, the sad circumstances organically brought us together in a moment of complete presence. But even when the circumstances are not that intense, a moment of gathering is never just a moment. It is what you make of it. There is always an opportunity for coherence, to blend together into the experience, to join into the moment. As a facilitator, you are the architect of that moment. You create and hold space in time for people to connect. You should never look at a gathering as just a random meet-up, or a waste of time. When there is even the slightest reason for people to spend time together, you can create a 'moment' for them.

As the architect of that moment, you have the privilege to foster presence and trust amongst the group members. You also can provide them with a sense of growth and progress. Being part of such a moment together is rewarding for people. It creates bonding and even happiness and motivation. Multiple feel-good hormones have been linked to sharing moments of co-creation together, like dopamine and serotonin, and the one that makes us feel trust: oxytocin. Feelings of trust are triggered when you see vulnerability and honesty in other people. Vulnerability and honesty do not only come across in your choice of words and tone of voice, but also through your appearance, through what you radiate. You cannot fake vulnerability. There is something intangible about the experience of trust. Often, you cannot really say why someone comes across as trustworthy and authentic. They just do.

Creating a level of trust at the start of any gathering is the most important thing when making it a success for everyone. It kickstarts the 'safe space' – or 'brave space' – where everyone feels comfortable to open up to each other. Trust is a great antidote to a narrow focus. Over the years, I have developed my own personal ritual for creating that trusting connection when people walk in the room or enter the virtual space. Through trial and error, I came to realize that what I emanate to people depends on how I feel about them, and about the situation at that moment. The practice I am about to explain will not appeal to everyone. If you love logic, facts and things that are tangible, this might sound too fluffy for you. But if you are convinced there is much more than meets the eye, you will find this interesting. What I am about to explain, is what I call 'heart hugs'. I have notied that when I practice them, it immediately changes the atmosphere when people enter the space.

Trust is a great antidote to a narrow focus.

HEART HUGS

So, how exactly do I do this? I start by making sure that I have finished preparing the session before it starts, so that I do not have to worry about timing, programming, tools, set-up or anything else. I can give my full attention to everyone entering the space. As the first person enters, I project a genuine feeling of appreciation for being given the chance to facilitate this person in this moment. In my mind, I often even say 'thank you for letting me be your facilitator today' while looking at that person, bringing up a feeling of gratitude. I repeat this each time another person enters the space. As I stir up these feelings of appreciation and gratitude towards each person in the group, I expand this feeling from my heart area. I imagine this feeling embracing each person as I focus on them. Hence, I call it a 'heart hug'. Whenever I notice a person who is distant, aggravated or stressed, or whenever I notice a type of personality that might be challenging for me, I try to tune up those feelings even more and embrace them with it.

I started doing this the moment I learned about the magnetizing effect of the energy in your heart area. It can be incredibly strong, especially combined with these appreciative emotions and the positive intentions of serving a group of people as a facilitator. When you focus on your heart area when giving heart hugs, you become more heart-centered, making you less likely to react to any stressors. It helps you to stay in the present moment. When people arrive and see you as a facilitator for the first time, they will notice you as the most 'present' person there. Everyone will unconsciously sense that it is safe to enter your space, and they will become more open without even noticing it. The state you are in at the moment when people enter your space will kickstart the 'safe space' or 'brave space'.

The state you are in at the moment when people enter your space will kickstart the 'safe space' or 'brave space'.

When I refer to space, I really mean that moment in time and space which you share with the participants of your gathering. Whether it is an online or offline gathering, you are holding space for everyone to open up and connect. I like to call it being 'the guardian of the space'. As a guardian of the space in which people co-create, you can generate that sense of belonging, of progress and growth. You can install all kinds of rituals for milestone moments. You can influence the way people communicate with each other, the language they use.

A MOMENT IS NEVER JUST A MOMENT

But should every shared moment be a facilitated shared moment? If there is a clear purpose a strong intention to build on whatever comes out of the gathering, there should be some level of facilitation. If it is just a pleasant get-together without the need for any results, it does not have to be facilitated. Just let it take you wherever it takes you and enjoy the ride. It can be a great or intense moment as well; it just does not need to have a purpose or outcome.

A moment is never just a moment.

The intense moment described at the start of this chapter did not need any facilitation, the outcome was already set in stone, and the purpose was not more than just being there. So, again, a moment is never just a moment, it is what you want to make of it, or what you need to make of it. And based on that, you can decide on the level of facilitation it needs. For myself, I refer to all moments where people gather to start with a purpose and end with a new start to 'do' something as moments of co-creation in the broadest sense of the word. Every moment of co-creation can benefit from some form of facilitation to make it count.

As a facilitator you can make co-creation count for all involved. You can be the architect of that moment, drawing everyone into a shared space of creativity. Your rituals generate a sense of progress and belonging. But there is a lot more you can do to make that moment count. You can become their guide, their conductor and their catalyst, blending a group of individuals into an individual group, thus lifting them up to their highest co-creative potential.

PRACTICAL ADVICE FOR THE HOLY TRINITY

The following chapters are filled with practical knowledge about how to apply facilitative leadership and connect people by their hands, their heads and their hearts. Guiding, Conducting and Catalysing are three separate takes on facilitation, and when applied simultaneously, they can drive coherence in a group of people. You can interpret them as three areas of competence that will help you to become an impactful facilitator. I have compiled these skills, tips and tricks over the years that I have practiced facilitation. Each chapter is wrapped up by a section I call 'Prepare for success'. Here, I will give you all kinds of tips and advice on how to come prepared so you can make each session a success.

I would like to invite you to build on them further and make them your own. Some skills will come to you naturally, you might even have a lot more experiences and tips to add. Others can take you out of your comfort zone and could become your area of development when you continue to take on opportunities to facilitate. As you gain more experience applying these competences, you can capture all your learnings in your notebook, your captain's log. Keeping track of my learnings have helped me to build this framework for my own development as a facilitator. Every day, I still learn something new about Guide, Conduct and Catalyse, and I write it down in my log. I believe that keeping track of your learnings in a structured way will help you to build your facilitative confidence.

Another thing that has really helped me, is my 'captaineering buddies' who I share and compare experiences with. Different perspectives on these competences will broaden your understanding of them. Sharing this book with other facilitation enthusiasts, can help you make captaineering buddies, people who understand the same facilitation concepts and want to share their learnings. Learning from each other will make facilitation even more exciting and effective.

Now catch the wind in your sails and expand your horizons …

6. Guide

How do you make sure people participate in your session?

Guiding is the practical side of facilitation. As facilitator it is your priority to ensure full participation. With participation, I mean that you get an unspoken agreement from everyone in the group that they will invest their time and energy in the session, in the moment. If the invitees are only participating with half of their effort or attention, there is no chance of making it worthwhile. There is no need to get an official spoken consent about participating. It would make them feel as if you are not expecting them to participate. This is an unspoken agreement. How people behave will tell you whether they are in the mood to fully participate. What does lack of participation look like?

Looking back at all the facilitation I have done at different organizations, there have only been a handful where everyone could stay until the end. Despite sending out calendar invites weeks in advance. These early leavers would take part, but at the same time they would be thinking about the next meeting. Often, they would send messages or emails and repeatedly look at the time. A slight feeling of guilt, or at least some sense of duty, would make them overly active in the session, trying to compensate for their absence a bit later. This overcompensation would then lead to unbalanced conversations in the session. The 'early leavers' would make some strong statements and contribute greatly, and then when they left, the rest would refer to their contribution like 'I believe that was Paul's point, I'm not sure what he meant by it. Let's leave it for now.'

All those 'Pauls' have one leg in the workshop and the other in their next meeting because their schedules are so packed. They are juggling so many tasks at the same time. Whatever the reason is, when people are overwhelmed, they often have a hard time focusing completely on the session.

While most people who are overwhelmed can still agree on the purpose of the gathering and actively participate, there are also apathetic people who are bored by the session and do not seem to feel the purpose is compelling enough to put in the effort. They lack enthusiasm and would rather be somewhere else. I have experienced people who barely contributed anything during a two-hour workshop. When I asked them for their opinion, they would take the chance to express that they did not see the point of the activity or conversation. Some of them would express this over and over again. I have had apathetic participants who did not even wait until I asked them a question before openly making clear that they did not see the point of participating.

I categorize these non-participants into the overwhelmed and the apathetic, and across these two you have the outspoken non-participants and the silent non-participants. All of them have one thing in common: they have stepped into the space with a narrow focus. The 'apathetics' bring up arguments like: 'We have already been through several workshops on these topics, and now we have to do another? When are things really going to start moving? Shouldn't we be doing things instead of talking about it all the time?' Another popular one is: 'We are already working on this, we know what to do, so why are we still spending time talking about it?' The silent apathetic group also feels this way as well, but they do not feel comfortable expressing it. They only contribute the bare minimum.

The overwhelmed people are always very apologetic and feel they are a victim of the circumstances. At the same time, they did prioritize something else above this session and that can never be hidden from the group with any apology. Their decisions about their priorities will always affect the group's sentiment about the session. The underlying message of their actions can be interpreted as 'I'm too important to spend all my time in this session, which obviously makes you less important when spending all your time here', or 'the other meeting was too important to cancel, which makes this one less important than my other meeting'. There are two things you need to solve as a facilitator. One is to maximize participation of overwhelmed or apathetic participants, and the other one is to minimize the effect they have on the participation level of the others.

AN APPEALING JOURNEY TO EMBARK ON

Over the years, I have learned that the level of participation is influenced by the way I handle time and the kind of journey I lay out for the team. People can still buy into the purpose of the gathering, and find the conversations enriching, but that does not necessarily mean that they will show the desired participative behavior. The series of activities you have planned, the journey you are asking them to embark on, plays a crucial role. I will refer to it as your 'narrative'. People will feel like joining in when they feel like the narrative is going somewhere. The different chapters in your story, or steps in your program, have to make sense to them. The best narratives are the ones that make people curious at first glance: what will come out of certain activities and conversations? There should be a balance between provocation and comfort.

There is always a starting point: the current status or situation. The end point is also clear: the goal you collectively want to achieve. When you share your agenda, it needs to clearly show the progress from the start to the end. You generally want to know what kind of movie you are going to watch, or what kind of book you will be reading before immersing yourself. You do not want to know the exact ending; that would ruin the suspense. But you want to know whether it is about solving crimes, an autobiography or a funny adventure with awkward situations. Within that journey, between the starting point and the ending, there will be important collaborative milestones, moments of consensus that build towards the end goal. The team will need to collectively shape, interpret and agree on crucial questions. For example: 'who are we dealing with?', 'what is the context?', 'how did we get here?', 'what is impacting this situation the most?', 'are sales and operations aligned?', 'do we really understand the customer's need?', 'what does the landscape look like now and how will it look in the near future?', etc.

So, in order to move forward towards a meaningful end goal with a team, you need to get through several steps that build on each other. These steps also always have a starting point and an end goal. A sense of meaning does not only come from having a clear narrative that connects the start and end of your session, but also every start and end in between.

The overall start and end, and the building blocks in between, always have a dynamic of opening and closing. When the session, or a specific step, opens, all participants need to understand where they are starting from. Is there any input or inspiration to get started? How does it connect to the previous step, and how are we using the previous

A good narrative pays close attention to moments of lift-off and closure; it fuels participation.

71

outcomes to build on further? To get everyone to fully participate, a stake needs to be put in the ground at every start, followed by a 'lift-off'. I like to call it lift-off, because every time you expect something from a group of people, you need to make sure they have the energy and a clear focus to 'fly'. I will explain how to make this happen further along in this chapter.

When the session closes, or when any step in between closes, there needs to be a collective feeling of closure. Everyone needs to feel at peace with the end result. It is like the moment of stretching after a good run, the moment you furl the sails after an adventure. A good closure at every step of the way juices up the group members to participate in the next step. It feels like progress.

TIME IS AN EXPERIENCE, AND IT IS A TRICKY ONE

Imagine having dinner with some good friends you have not seen in a while: the conversation is enjoyable, the food tastes wonderful, and everyone laughs about some shared memories: time flies. A few hours seem to have passed by in a flash. But can you recall any instance when you were waiting to receive some important news, or maybe your child or pet went missing? I remember shopping in a large clothing store with my wife and son. It was absolutely packed. The atmosphere was chaotic. My oldest son was just over three years old, and without us noticing, he ran off on an adventure. We could not find him anywhere. The minutes felt like hours while worst case scenarios ran through my mind at high speed. Finally, I heard shop staff announcing a boy asking for his parents at the counter. It felt like being pulled out of a horrific vacuum. In this moment, the world around me moved forward at a hectic and confusing pace, and my world just came to a standstill looking for that little person who means the world to me. Everything I was thinking and doing immediately stopped and every moment of searching felt like an eternity.

As the owner of time, being the guardian of the space, you have the power to give your participants the gift of time.

When you look at the time on your phone or watch, it is a fact. But when you interpret that time indication within your context, it becomes part of your experience. It might add to your rushed feeling, or it might increase your feeling of boredom or anticipation. Our agendas are often so crowded with things we need to do that time has become – mosty – a pressurizing factor. Time feels like a fixed frame restricting the amount of things we can do in a day.

As a facilitator, when you are holding space for people to share thoughts, to co-create new conclusions or new strategies, you are the owner of time. The participants are taking part in your moment and you have the power to create the experience of time for them. This is often a heavily underestimated privilege. You have the power to give your participants the gift of time, while time these days is often a precious and scarce asset, a luxury.

When I am facilitating a workshop in a high-paced organizational environment and I tell the participants to just take a bit of time to comfortably think about the topic before discussing it, they seem to feel strangely relieved. They all seem to be wired to take the least amount of time possible to do anything. When you create an experience that makes them feel like time is on their side, it can be the key to open them up and relax their minds. The comfortable experience of time can help participants to lean into the moment. It is a very powerful tool to earn their trust, because you are the owner of something which is very scarce to them. They will follow your lead if you fill in their time comfortably and meaningfully.

The appeal of your narrative and the experience of time are intertwined. Your narrative is a program that the team works through in time. It will be very hard to create a comfortable experience of time if the program is too packed with difficult discussions, activities and decisions. If you know upfront that the team is far from aligned on the topics at hand, you need to make sure the expectations about the output are realistic. Or plan for enough time for them to find their common ground.

Another pitfall to watch out for is being too focused on creating a comfortable time experience and ending up at only halfway through your program, when it is too late to fix it. When you are building your sequence of 'lift-off's' and 'closures', always imagine how much time would be needed to reach each ending, so there is enough time to comfortably get lift-off for a next step. This is one of the hardest things to do in preparation, because you might not know all team members very well and you have not seen them working together yet. Even so, you need to try to get a sense of how much time they will need to get to their decisions and conclusions.

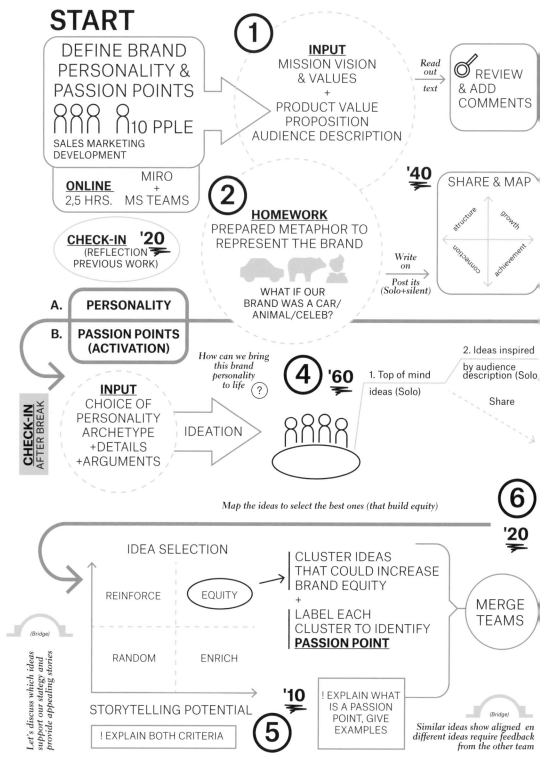

START

DEFINE BRAND PERSONALITY & PASSION POINTS

10 PPLE
SALES MARKETING DEVELOPMENT

ONLINE 2,5 HRS. | MIRO + MS TEAMS

CHECK-IN '20 (REFLECTION PREVIOUS WORK)

A. PERSONALITY

B. PASSION POINTS (ACTIVATION)

CHECK-IN AFTER BREAK

① **INPUT**
MISSION VISION & VALUES
+
PRODUCT VALUE PROPOSITION AUDIENCE DESCRIPTION

Read out text → REVIEW & ADD COMMENTS

② **HOMEWORK**
PREPARED METAPHOR TO REPRESENT THE BRAND

WHAT IF OUR BRAND WAS A CAR/ ANIMAL/CELEB?

'40 **SHARE & MAP**
structure | growth
connection | achievement

Write on Post its (Solo+silent)

INPUT
CHOICE OF PERSONALITY ARCHETYPE +DETAILS +ARGUMENTS

How can we bring this brand personality to life ?

④ '60

IDEATION

1. Top of mind ideas (Solo)

2. Ideas inspired by audience description (Solo
Share

Map the ideas to select the best ones (that build equity)

⑥ '20

IDEA SELECTION

REINFORCE | EQUITY → | CLUSTER IDEAS THAT COULD INCREASE BRAND EQUITY
+
LABEL EACH CLUSTER TO IDENTIFY **PASSION POINT**

RANDOM | ENRICH

MERGE TEAMS

STORYTELLING POTENTIAL '10

! EXPLAIN BOTH CRITERIA

⑤ ! EXPLAIN WHAT IS A PASSION POINT, GIVE EXAMPLES

(Bridge)

Let's discuss which ideas support our stategy and provide appealing stories

(Bridge)

Similar ideas show aligned en different ideas require feedback from the other team

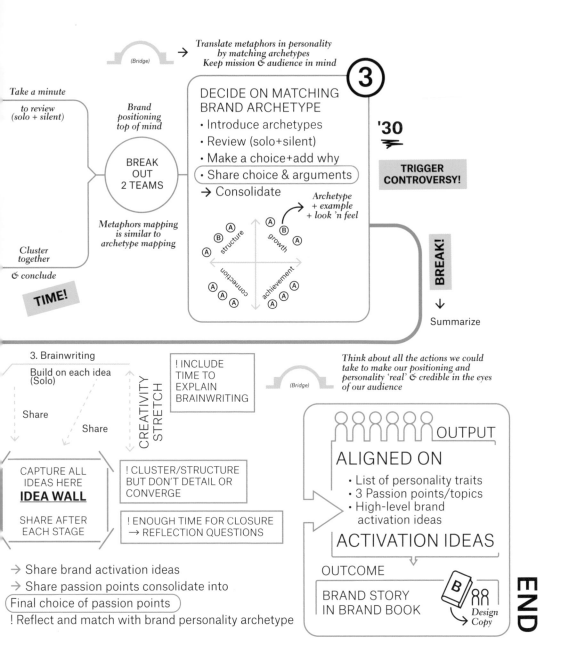

Fig. 2 A sketch created for a Brand Activation workshop. It does not include all the details, as that would be too intricate to show as an example, but it has the most important elements. It was not drawn for other people to see, so in general I do not put any effort into making it look beautiful. It is the act of sketching it out that helps my thought process. Thus, I create the session and imagine what it is like to experience as a participant.

Any thoughts about pitfalls, instructions, tools, points of attention, I add to the drawing. When finished, I stare at it for a while, maybe add some more thoughts here and there, and then I put it aside and create the high-level agenda. This kind of sketching is intended only to support your thought process, not to communicate the structure of the workshop.

And if you are not sure, it is always better to plan more than enough time and prepare some trigger questions to ramp up the speed of conversation. I will tell you all about trigger questions in the next chapter.

Now let's deep dive into some practices which can drive participation in your session.

'GUIDING' PRACTICES TO ENCOURAGE PARTICIPATION

There are three 'Guiding' practices. These three aspects have helped me manage participation. Before we dig into these practices, let me point out again that this book is meant to be divergent. I am sharing my experiences with you to trigger your interest and imagination so you can build on them further. And as you build, you will learn to shape this 'guiding' as a facilitator.

1. **Narrating the journey:** I invest a lot of energy in sketching narratives as if they were journeys.

2. **Timing timelessness:** I am also very conscious of creating a nice experience of time.

3. **Preparing for 'lift-off':** My instructions can create lift-offs or landings, or or in worst case crashes.

Your narrative, your time experience and your instructions provide structure to your session. These three elements help you to gain trust. Let's examine them in more detail.

1. Narrating the journey

Your narrative is about bridging several building blocks from the starting point to the end goal. It is not only a list of agenda points; your narrative explains how to get past different milestones to arrive at the destination. It includes clear starting points, ways of processing and concluding together to arrive at decisive closure moments. It is a journey with obstacles to overcome together. In other words, it should not only be clear to everyone what the milestones are, it should also be obvious what bridges and roads will get the team from each milestone to the next.

Your narrative is also the framework you have in your head. And within that framework you guide the participants to fill in the gaps. You are guiding them to build a captivating story with a valuable ending. If you are covering several topics in a meeting, the meeting could consist of a couple of stories. If you are tackling one big challenge with a clear end goal in a workshop, it could be one big story. In any case, the story is always unique. It is the 'fingerprint' of the gathering. A gathering of people is always a unique moment, and the story or stories that are co-created, are always unique as well.

Despite the popularity of methodologies, there is no one-size-fits-all method to build a good narrative. Your narrative, the tools you apply to trigger thought processes, or any model you apply, should always be reshaped to suit this unique composition of people and context. Each building block in your narrative, to guide the creation of the story, should be meticulously created and placed.

I always start with a rough sketch, drawing the starting point with some keywords around input, invitees and set-up. Then I draw the ending point with some key words around the end state and goal. Then I start drawing the roadmap with milestone moments in between, and I literally draw bridges explaining the handovers between the closures and lift-offs, jumping from one building block to the next. I also sketch some tools or techniques if necessary, to guide the thought processes within each building block. And then I often stare at it and add some extra points of attention, like a painter staring at their painting and gradually adding some strokes here and there.

As I am staring at the narrative, I envision what the group dynamics will be like going through this journey, and I imagine what my key instructions will be, and which pitfalls might occur. Basically, I am bringing this journey to life in my mind before it happens. If I know the team already, I will sketch in some potential differences in perspective, so I know where to emphasize conducting efforts (I will explain what conducting is on page 99). If I do not know the team, I tap into my memory base of how teams usually behave during this type of journey. While I am doing this,

I keep in mind the time experience, and I already draw in time requirements at different stages.

Sketching will help you to become a better guide. When you have overwhelmed or apathetic people in your sessions, you will easily be able to remind them the value of each step when questioned, because you have a holistic vision of the full journey visually imprinted in your brain. If they question the value of the gathering, you will be able to quickly summarize the highlights of what you will do and why. If they question a step in your narrative, you will be able to answer how it relates to the next steps or how it builds on the previous one with clear argumentation. It prepares you to earn all the necessary trust, even from less participatory team members. See **Fig. 2** on page 74–75, an example of a sketched out narrative.

THE JOURNEY IS IN YOUR HEAD

On the other hand, and this might sound contradictory, having a visualization of the journey in your memory also provides you with all the necessary flexibility to adapt your narrative. If you have a detailed framework in your head, it is easy to imagine what effect any changes to the program might have on the full journey of the team. It will make it possible for you to easily take into account any comments or suggestions from the team and reshape the journey on-the-spot.

Not too long ago, I built a workshop to articulate the value proposition of a new offer at an organization. At a certain point during the workshop, someone shared a PDF detailing a value proposition for that same offer. I was caught by surprise. This proposition was already created and discussed in an earlier workshop and my contact person had not been aware of this work. It was quite alarming, we had just arrived at the point in my narrative where we would start building the value proposition, and now that activity seemed completely pointless. I was about to lose all trust, and participants had enough reasons to disengage. I had to turn things around quickly. Before doing anything else, I acknowledged to the group that I did not have this information before. Then I suggested to have a ten-minute break so I had some time to incorporate it into our workshop.

Anything unforeseen can be turned into an opportunity.

During the break, I refined the upcoming activity. When everyone came back from the break,

I asked them to put up some brown paper up on the wall and I asked them to think about reasons why they would change certain wordings in the existing proposition. I split the group into two teams, and both sides had to review and build arguments. Then I brought them together in a fun conversational battle to defend their own new version of the proposition and share their arguments. Both teams got excited while debating about the wording of the proposition. Their mission was to make peace in the end and to write down all the compromises necessary to achieve that peace. It resulted in a better proposition, with great arguments to underpin the wording and with full buy-in from all the participants. It even generated some more energy and enthusiasm to continue building on the proposition. I would not have achieved the same result if they had worked with the proposition from the other workshop without evaluating it first. Trust was restored – even increased. It strengthens my belief that anything unforeseen can be turned into an opportunity.

Adapting might sound like the obvious thing to do. But when you have spent lots of time and energy to create a good narrative, the last thing you want to hear is that your session – or any step – is not valuable enough to participate in. Most facilitators try to ignore comments from narrow-focused critics, or they spend too much time defending their approach and explaining why it is valuable. Often the phrase 'trust the process' is used to neutralize pushback. But pushback is never neutralized by ignoring or blocking it. It can lead to a hijacking of the session, ending up in a battle between the facilitator and the critic. Worst-case scenario: the critic influences the group's opinion, thus getting support from the group. In that case, the facilitator is in a tough spot, losing the trust of the group. And trust is the most valuable currency for a facilitator. You can easily tell when you are losing trust: it happens when people start to mimic the other person. They will start to behave similarly to the critic or the apathetic person, and they will stop sharing your enthusiasm about the session.

Obviously, this is a situation you want to avoid at all times. But, as a facilitator guiding the group to their desired end goal, it is your duty to take all opinions into account. Whether you like it or not, you need to verify whether there is a valuable argument or some information you might have missed. A piece of information which would actually help the group to achieve the end goal better or quicker. If so, you need to incorporate it in your program of activities. This means you need to listen deeply – also to the critic – to check whether there is anything to improve the journey on the spot. When you are evaluating, you need to be in service of the whole team. It is not just your opinion. You need to break it open to the full group and involve everyone in the decision. Take into account any suggestions, feedback or critique. If the group agrees on a valuable point, it is your job to smoothly incorporate it and possibly change the course of your narrative. You might remember that vulnerability and honesty generate trust. This is the moment to avoid becoming defensive but to go with the flow of things and stay open. Your participants will not blame you if you change things based on their input. They will also appreciate the fact that you are honest about not knowing everything and still learning about new input. This sort of situation can even boost their trust in you, especially when you gain the trust of critics.

DO A BRUCE LEE

I have labeled this the 'Bruce Lee move'. Like in martial arts, this move is about not meeting force with force, but about harnessing your opponent's energy and using it to your advantage. Take the energy and use it to change it for the better. Never block people's feedback or criticism, because they will either disconnect and cause disconnect in other participants, or they will manifest their opinion even stronger, thus hijacking the session. When it happens, just make an awesome Bruce Lee sound in your head (yes, only in your head) and use the energy to the advantage of the group. Be flexible and stay open so the best ideas for adaptations can come to the surface.

2. Timing timelessness

To ensure a safe space where every individual organically blends into a productive collective, you need to create a comfortable experience of time. This means that people feel they have the time to gather their thoughts, express them in the group and understand everyone's perspective to collectively build towards a common understanding.

Over the past years, I have learned that the start of the session is the crucial moment to shape the time experience. When at the start, the participants cannot smoothly lean into the gathering to understand the context, purpose and team composition, they will easily get propelled into a more narrowed focus, or even into a state of anxiety. I always start slowly to let everyone enter the shared moment at their own pace. I build in a check-in moment, asking a personal question, and I have a short introduction round. Even if they already know each other. I try to create some enjoyable moments of smiles and hopefully even laughter, which will relax everyone's mind. Any instructions or explanations at the start should be especially easy to follow and to the point.

I have been in meetings where people were immediately thrown into an overly complicated PowerPoint slide in a small font with a lot of squares, arrows, colors and descriptions, just to convince everyone of a point. Hence, it is called PowerPoint. The slide is immediately followed by a discussion and, not surprisingly, everyone has a hard time agreeing. When the lead of the meeting feels under time pressure and starts bombarding everyone immediately with overwhelming content, they overlook the effects of rushing people into the moment instead of allowing time for everyone. Ironically, it takes more time to manage all the triggered discussions than the time it takes to have a slow, comfortable start avoiding a lot of pressure and friction.

SPINNING THE WHEEL

At every 'start' during a session, the participants need to get the time to digest 'closure' of the previous step and get ready for the next one. It might even be a good idea to install a break followed by a new moment to check in or reflect. You are giving the participants time to lean into the session again and focus on the next step. As a facilitator, it is always a good idea to build a list of rituals to accommodate lift-offs and moments of closure. These rituals can help you in creating a comfortable time experience for your participants. They will also shape your personal style of facilitation. A ritual can be as simple as giving everyone a couple of minutes to silently and individually recap how they have accomplished getting this far.

Provide a quiet spot – or quiet moment – for participants to reflect and then ask them to give a thumbs up when they feel ready to move on. This simple

Remember, it is often those little processing moments that avoid time-consuming discussions or confusion later on.

ritual can work wonders when building a comfortable time experience. If you label your ritual with a specific name, you will build a new habit for your participants. I labeled this ritual of silent reflection at the time of closure 'spinning', like the spinning wheel on an Apple device which indicates that it is processing. Remember, it is often those little processing moments, allowing everyone to catch up, catch their breath and prepare the next move forward, that avoid time-consuming discussions or confusion later on.

Summarizing: a slow start helps everyone to recalibrate their focus into the moment, a slow end helps everyone to consolidate and prepare for the next step, the next lift-off. As long as the start and the end are slow, people feel comfortable with a faster pace in between.

YOU SHAPE THE EXPERIENCE OF TIME

Another important aspect to consider when creating a comfortable time experience is the way you give time indications. They provide extra structure for the participants. Without it, they can get lost in conversation or lack a feeling of progress. But the way you indicate time will shape their experience of time. Below are my two rules of thumb when it comes to giving time indications. I am sure you can add several more in your own captain's log once you start paying more attention to how you use time indications in your sessions.

Rule of thumb: HOW. I always use wording that sounds positive and generates a sense of time abundance.

'We have a good half hour to come to an agreement, giving us sufficient time to share our thoughts. I suggest we use the first five minutes to structure our thoughts individually, just to make sure everyone can gather their thoughts beforehand. If we do end up needing more than the half hour, don't worry, I'll make sure we will have that time available and still finish all the other things we need to do.'

It is important to keep in mind that you want people to jump into collecting their thoughts with an open focus. If they do not feel pressured, thoughts will actually come to their minds more quickly. If you use time pressure, it might decrease their creativity and they may only come up with one thing to add, or even nothing. If you use time pressure, it will take you more time to get more thoughts and ideas out of them. Like in this example:

'We only have half an hour to complete this, and we really need to stick to our timing because we still have so much to accomplish during the rest of this meeting. So please start writing down your thoughts as quickly as you can, so we can start sharing them and reach an agreement.'

Here, it is the facilitator expressing their anxiety about not being able to finish in time, thus creating anxiety in others. Although it feels contradictory, the relaxed minds in the first example will be more productive than the tense narrowed minds under time pressure. They will also reach a conclusion much quicker, having more options to consider and more openness towards each other.

On a sidenote, some brainstorm techniques use time pressure to nurture creativity. Using time pressure does not necessarily mean that people feel pressured into a survival mode. When it is applied in a gamified way, like a fun competition to add as many ideas as possible within a fixed timeframe, it actually may increase their creativity. Applying pressure does not always result in negative feelings of pressure. Only when people feel 'threatened' in a way, their mind will narrow.

Rule of thumb: WHEN. I never wait until the last minute to give a time indication. I always give time indications shortly after the start of an activity or discussion, or somewhere in the middle. This gives you the chance to say things like: 'We are a couple of minutes into our activity, and we are already making some really good progress.' You give the group a sense of progress and some encouragement. If you give time indications towards the very end, it can sound like: 'We have one minute left.' Participants will just ignore it, or it will pressure them, blocking their final thoughts. Instead, ask them to indicate where they notice gaps or things that have not been discussed, to trigger some last thoughts right before the end.

UNEXPECTED BREAKS ARE THE BEST BREAKS

Another tip to create a comfortable time experience is to give unexpected breaks. Just allocate a bucket of time to breaks and use it whenever you feel it makes most sense. Maybe the energy level is low, or a comment from a critical participant undermines your narrative (take the time to talk with this person during the break, not openly in group). Or you need to create a sense of closure or a window of time to reassess the rest of your program and make some changes. Usually participants love breaks, and when they get them as an unexpected gift, online or offline, they usually perceive time as abundant.

I always prefer frequent shorter breaks to a few longer ones. Often, people get into emails or other distractions when you provide longer breaks. It will take you quite some time to get them back into the moment afterwards. It is always a great idea to turn breaks into one of your rituals. For example, when I announce a break, I also suggest some things they could do to indulge or relax a bit. I might recommend stepping out on the balcony and take some deep breaths while enjoying the scenery, or to take the time and make a nice cappuccino. I also encourage them not to spend every break on email or social media, but to allow for some natural mind wandering. You could even ask them to think about something fun to do during breaks, and when they come back you have a sharing round as a check-in. The point is, if they do not enjoy the break time, they will have less of a feeling of time abundance. And by now you know that a feeling of time abundance keeps them open, relaxed and participative.

I have labeled my own quick breaks of mind wandering as 'blank space', referring to an empty moment in between things. I often apply blank space even when I am not facilitating. With a couple of minutes of blank space, I allow myself to just be, without thinking or imagining anything. I only pay attention to my breathing, or I just try and listen to all the different noises in the moment without defining them. Or I might just look at colors and shapes without contemplation. Of course, thoughts will keep popping up in my head, I just do not pay any attention to them.

To conclude this part on time experience, I would like to emphasize that flexibility in your timing is essential. When you are sketching out the narrative, and you are adding in time allocations, you need to identify yourself with the team to understand whether the time allocations will work. Think about how familiar they are with the content and topics, but also how diverse the group might be and how much time they might need to find common ground. Also consider how familiar they are with the tools and thought processes you are asking them to take part in. Once you feel comfortable about the journey they will embark on, and about the amount of time they have to do

I have never been in a session where the timing ran perfectly. And it shouldn't.

so, memorize it as your framework. Your sketch will help you to visually memorize it. With the timeframe clearly in your mind, you can easily adapt it on the spot. If some activities take longer, you immediately foresee the impact it has on other parts of your programme, and you can adjust accordingly.

I have never been in a session where the timing ran perfectly. And it shouldn't. When valuable conversations are taking place you want to give them the necessary time to finish. Your mission is to make sure they do not have to worry one bit about the timing. They need to be confident that you got this.

3. Prepare for lift-off

This practical side of facilitation is about structuring the session in such a way that people feel like participating. An appealing narrative can help all participants to join the journey of the session together. Creating a comfortable and encouraging time experience pulls them in even more. The way you give instructions then makes or breaks the flow.

There were moments during facilitation when I went completely overboard when giving instructions. It is not good captaineering when you are drowning in your own words. For some reason I did not only explain what the first step should be, I also explained how that would lead to the rest of the activities, how everything was connected, and I even threw in a big explanation about the 'why'. After a while people could not remember how I had started my story. I could not even remember myself. Their faces started to look more and more puzzled. They just frowned or stared at me. These expressions told me I was not doing a great job at explaining things, and I then would try to fix it explaining even more, gasping for air, drowning in words. Ah, memories …

Participants feel more comfortable when they immediately understand what is expected of them. It is best to chop up all explanations into small relevant bits and drip-feed it to keep momentum going. Instructions can make or break the flow. Long-winded explanations covering too many topics take a lot of energy to take in. The last thing you want to do is to deplete your crew of energy right before they have to start 'performing' together.

Your choice of words can keep momentum going. Be mindful of the kind of language your team is used to. If you are working in an informal setting with people who have fun with each other every day, there is no need to use formal language. If you are working in a very formal setting with foreign politicians, dealing with different cultures and covering sensitive matters, you want to be more formal and diplomatic in your choice of words. As a facilitator, you need to empathize with your participants and adapt your style to make sure that your instructions resonate with them.

If I facilitate a workshop with a Marketing team and I use their jargon in my instructions, for example 'Net Promotor Score' or 'Inbound Marketing', I will be more easily accepted as part of the in-group. I will earn their trust more easily. The same thing happens in technology or banking. Learning some basic terminology relevant to the gathering will help to drive participation.

CALL THEM BY THEIR NAME

At the start of every meeting or workshop I facilitate, I always greet everyone with their first name, and I double-check whether I am pronouncing it correctly. It is such an important trust-generating tool that it is absolutely worth the effort to get it right from the start. And it does impact the feelings of trust if you keep mispronouncing someone's name. It is not always easy to know which name to use. Like when someone is called Xin-Chen but is addressed as Jen by her colleagues. Or when someone has a three- to four-word name, and I don't know whether to call out all of them or only one. And then, which one? Using the right first name is a big deal. When you can refer to what a participant mentioned earlier in the workshop while calling them by their name, it generates trust and keeps them in the game. You can apply it strategically by often calling out people who are less participative. It helps to keep them in the moment.

GIVE INSTRUCTIONS AS IF IT WAS A PEP-TALK

I compare giving instructions with pep talks. Conciseness, a good choice of words and a personal approach are key characteristics of a powerful pep talk. It should energize and prepare someone for what is to come. Especially when I pay attention to the right tone of voice.
I have experienced facilitators who naturally have a very mellow tone of voice. It is pleasant to listen to, it makes everyone feels relaxed. But after a while it becomes monotonous. It feels likes the energy level of the team

becomes stagnant. There is no a drop in energy, but no peak either. People participate, but they have to keep themselves motivated. I have also experienced facilitators who talk very fast, with a high-pitched voice throughout a complete session. People will definitely be awake, but it will also wear them out after a while. At first, they are energized by the sense of urgency coming from the tone of voice. But after a while, they become immune to the sense of urgency – even when things become urgent.

The voice of a facilitator is an incredibly important tool.

The voice of a facilitator is an incredibly important tool. It can put everyone at ease, get everyone to focus, and stir up the team to quicken the pace. Especially in an online environment, your voice is one of the most important means of communication. Just ask yourself this: if you don't sound excited about the next step or topic, how can you expect anyone else to feel excited? When giving instructions, I play a lot with my voice and my facial expression. I deepen my voice when I want to create suspense and get everyone's close attention. I become louder when I need to wake everyone up and when I am about to create a 'lift-off' to get them started with an activity. I use silences to give participants time to think about what I just said. This helps them to digest everything before I move on to the next sentence of explanation. I will come back to this in the next chapter about conducting.

Especially when you are not part of the in-group, when you seem to come from a completely different background, it is absolutely crucial to sound confident when giving instructions. Avoid hesitation in your voice, because it will make your participants trust you less. When I am facilitating a group of people I never met before, in a company where I have never been before, maybe even in a foreign country, my voice is the first thing that makes a real connection. You might think it is your appearance, but it is actually the sound of your voice, along with the words you use. The length of your explanations can decrease the impact of your voice. If you keep it confident, to the point, using familiar jargon and calling people by their names from time to time, you will build trust. This will help you to establish yourself as a facilitative leader.

Now, get ready for some practical advice on how to prepare for successful guiding.

How do you prepare for successful guiding as a facilitator? There are three items you need to spend a good amount of time on:

1. Managing expectations on what needs to be produced during the session;
2. carefully designing and testing your narrative, and;
3. outlining the available input for the session.

By doing these three things, you will be gearing yourself up to be an excellent guide.

Managing expectations

Almost every time I am asked to facilitate a workshop at a larger organization, I need to tone down the expectations. A workshop is designed to bring a diverse group of people together to build on each other's perspectives in order to get to an agreed view on things.

It is important to make a clear distinction between *output*, *outcome* and *impact*. A facilitated workshop or meeting generates output. Output can be a range of decisions, an approach, a summary, focus points, high-level solutions, etc. Executing an output generates an outcome. Any gathering of people has an output rather than an outcome, simply because it is really difficult for a group of people to develop something in detail while conversing about it. For example, you can decide on a new strategic line of cars in a workshop, but it takes time and work to actually build a first prototype.

Almost every time I am asked to facilitate a workshop at a larger organization, I need to tone down the expectations.

When I get briefed to design and facilitate a workshop, I often need to point out that the output can only be some kind of direction, a high-level agreement on certain topics based on co-creative efforts. The desired outcome will only happen if there is enough ownership to build on the output afterwards.

While the output is the direct product of the conversations and activities, and the outcome is the intended – or unintended – consequence of building on the output, the impact is a result of a series of outcomes over time. They are the fundamental direct and indirect effects of all activities over a long-term period. Impact is often related to long-term strategic goals. Outcome can immediately build on the output. Impact can be the evolved culture, the sustainable practices, the new product line, or the high NPS score which is eventually the result of multiple outcomes.

To manage expectations, you need to determine which type of output is necessary to build an outcome afterwards, and whether this outcome needs to feed into a desired impact over time. By aligning all key stakeholders upfront on expectations, you empower yourself to guide a team to clearly endorsed and realistic goals. This way, you will avoid unrealictic expectations of generating outcomes or even impact from just a single gathering of people.

Prototype your sketches

I never just create a detailed planning of a gathering in Excel or Power-Point. I always take out my markers and colored pencils to sketch the journey. Like a captain rolling out the map on the table in the captain's cabin, taking notes and measurements to prepare for the journey, I invite you to sketch out the flow and look at it from different sides and perspectives.

The act of drawing and sketching builds your confidence about the approach. It allows you to imagine how to give instructions at different stages, and it helps you to foresee when you need to manage the energy in the group.

There are different steps you need to take when sketching the narrative:

1. Starting point of the session with the purpose, the team, the input.
2. Ending point of the session with the output (and the desired outcome to be created afterwards).

3. Islands of activity or conversation in between, adding the goal, the tool, the time and the conversational dynamic (this can be done solo, in pairs, with the whole group …).
4. The bridges connecting the islands with rituals: a 'lift-off' with first a check-in and some points of attention for the instructions and a 'closure' moment, identifying the expected output of the activity.

Consider this sketch to be your rough prototype to test with key stakeholders. If I am not sure about certain elements, I first visit some fellow captains to get a second opinion. Every captain has their own set of tricks. If the session requires some serious stakeholder management, I might create a simple version to share with key stakeholders to get their buy-in upfront. This simple version could be a list of activities in an Excel sheet, indicating the different steps and the output of each step, building towards the end goal. If I am not familiar with the participants, I might share the flow in detail with the project owner, who may be able give me some feedback on feasibility based on the experience, expertise and personalities in the team.

1. After testing my prototype, I add notes on where pitfalls might occur in the flow. These are potential risks that may decrease participation or even disengagement.
2. Prototyping your narrative in advance will give you more confidence about providing the right structure to your session in order to generate trust.

Become part of the in-group

Every time a group of people decide to sit together to achieve something, there is a history, or at least some context that led to this point. There will be all kinds of variables that influence the nature of that shared moment. Some variables can provide very valuable and relevant information to understand the starting point of the session. Use this information to create an inspirational lift-off at the start. Providing some extra perspectives and stories can reinforce the purpose of the session. If the amount of information is extensive, it can be provided as a pre-read to gain knowledge about some facts, technology, trends, etc.

When I foresee that participants will come in with preconceived notions about the topic or challenge, I ask them to first pre-read articles or blogs that disrupt their fixed way of thinking. I might even bring in someone to give them a presentation with an unexpected view on the subject matter. That will soften up their rigid opinions and views on reality, and it will prepare them to be further inspired by each other's perspectives.

Coming up with pre-work or figuring out what the best inspiration would be for a 'lift-off', helps me to get a better understanding of the participant's language and context. It allows me to become part of their in-group. When I get myself acquainted with the input, I try to generate as much empathy as possible, imagining what is important to the group, what motivates them, what they are faced with in their work, and what this gathering means to them.

Even if you are very familiar with the topic, it still makes sense to go through any input yourself, because it will give you a better empathic understanding about what it is like to be a participant in your session.

A TRUSTWORTHY GUIDE

Participation is your first priority as a facilitator. Trust is the currency. Building your narrative, leading a group of people through the narrative, owning time, pep-talking to gain momentum, and all the preparation will turn you into a trustworthy guide. When you achieve a good level of participation, you can use that focus and energy of the group to tune up their engagement to the moment, to the other participants and to the cause.

Captain's Log

Now, it's up to you to start working on your captain's log. Do not be afraid to experiment…do not be afraid to make mistakes. It is all part of jour journey. Try out the Bruce Lee move in your next session. Experiment with an empathy check-in and see what happens. Play with the techniques explained below. And when you do, note down the impact, the return, the surprises and even the struggles that you experience.

When you understand the purpose, the team of participants and the type of output, you are ready to sketch your narrative. Take a blank piece of paper, preferably A3, grab your marker, find a quiet spot and …

Step 1: Draw the starting point of your gathering, include a reference to the input, invited roles and characters and some characteristics of the space (online or offline).

Step 2: Then, draw the end point and leave enough space in between, include an element referencing the type of output and the preferred end state of the team (for example: aligned, a pledge to action, task forces, etc.).

Step 3: In between the start and end, add the building blocks of the journey. For each building block, describe the lift-off, the goal of the activity, any references to tools or conversational dynamics (pairs, sub-teams, group conversation) and finalize with an indication of the type of closure (reflection: what went well, what didn't, feedback on the work, a recap of the journey so far).

Step 4: Connect each closure and lift-off of the next stage with a bridge and add some notes to remind yourself how to explain the build-up towards the end.

Step 5: Take a step back and run through all the steps.
Highlight where you expect controversy and how you can 'mine' for it. For example, you can split the group into smaller teams with specifically selected participants and a specific assignment to prepare their perspective for a group discussion. Or you add some provocative questions to ask at certain moments in the journey.
Highlight the pitfalls in a different color, like red. For example, the moments when you break out, when a speaker needs to join in, when an activity might cause overwhelm, when you might run out of time, etc.

Step 6: Finalize the sketch by adding the time blocks. This is the last step, because you need to take into account that controversies and pitfalls might mess up your time schedule. Make sure to add some buffers when certain important moments in the journey take longer. For example, position your breaks strategically after activities which may take longer than expected. But never compromise a slower start or end of your gathering. These are crucial elements for delivering a comfortable time experience.

Experiment 2 / EMPATHY CHECK-IN

When you need the team to switch perspectives, in order to ensure human-centered output, try out a slow start with an empathy check-in. This can be either at the start of your session or at the start of a new stage. Gather the team around or ask them to keep the online video platform open on their screen and …

a) Start by calming everyone down and have them lean into the moment. Use a warm voice, talk slowly and remind everyone how valuable it is to understand the reality of the *person(a).

b) Briefly provide some context, describe a relevant situation, for example 'our persona has some friends over for dinner and wants to prepare … using our …' and ask them to imagine what they would feel.

c) Let them think about what this person(a) would say about their situation to their closest friends.

d) Allow the participants to take two minutes to silently become that person(a).

e) Start a sharing round: ask the first person to explain the person(a)s thoughts and feelings, acting it out as if they were that person(a), using words this person(a) would use and even using a different voice. Then ask the first participant to assign the next until everyone has shared their interpretation.

f) When everyone has shared their point of view, call out similarities and contradictions. Spend five more minutes for the team to comment on the contradictions.

g) Thank everyone for openly and vividly sharing their interpretations and use the similarities and contradictions to build a bridge to the next stage of the session.

Acting out an empathic interpretation can have an eye-opening effect on a team. To make this work, all participants need to feel comfortable with each other, because 'becoming' the person(a) means showing vulnerability. It requires a good level of trust in the facilitator. Make sure

you time your empathy check-in correctly and avoid any peer pressure
to force participants into the spotlight when they are not ready yet.

   *   person(a): a person, or a group of people, who has become the
subject of the session, the workshop or the conversation. The
focus of the problem-solving activities or the inspiration to come
up with the desired output.

Experiment 3 / BRUCE LEE

When a strong statement, criticism or negative emotions from a participant threaten to disrupt the session, be like water …

- Welcome the attack: hold the space and direct everyone's attention to the input.
- Observe the attack: assess the 'incoming' on potential disruption
and opportunities.
- Become fluid and flexible: activate an emotion of appreciation
for this input.
- Take the energy: acknowledge the input as a contribution.
- Harness the energy: highlight the relevance of the statement
to the overall purpose and current activity or conversation
(if unclear, ask a few clarifying questions first).
- Change the course of the energy: ask the group to comment,
integrating it into the current thinking, and if possible, make it
actionable.
- Observe the impact: check whether the consensus matches the
intentions and expectations of the participant.
- Find balance again: recap or reflect to achieve closure.

This might look elaborate. But it happens quickly if you just remember
to never block the input of a participant, even if it has a potentially disruptive effect. And always tap into the collective intelligence to decide
on what to do with the input, break it open for the group to interpret
and decide. Your role as a facilitator is to serve the group to reach the
best decisions, not to judge or defend.

Experiment 4 / ENCOURAGING TIME INDICATIONS

When the team needs more clarity on available time to participate comfortably in a discussion or activity …

> **How:** use words like 'more than enough', 'take all the time you need' and 'not even halfway'. When participants feel that time is on their side, it will generate a sense of abundance, which encourages an open focus.
> **When:** provide indications at the start and in the first half. Avoid mentioning time indications in the last minutes of an exercise, only ask to finalize any last thoughts or finetune an ending statement.

The trick is to refer to time when there is still quite some time left. When there is no more time left, you only use words to wrap things up. If you would say 'only one minute left', you generate a sense of scarcity, leading to a narrow focus. By saying 'finish your last sentence' you indicate that the activity is coming to an end, without pointing out that time is short.

Experiment 5 / NAME-CALLING

When participants are distracted, need acknowledgement, are expected to contribute, should engage in conversation, could use a sense of belonging, … when you need to make it more personal or get immediate attention, call them by their first name. But make sure you pronounce it correctly by: **welcoming** each participant with their first name right at the **start** of your session when the participant **enters** the space. **Ask** each person whether you pronounced the name correctly, and **remember** the right pronunciation when using their names in the session

Your name is the most important word in your life. Being called by your first name always catches your attention. But when it is pronounced incorrectly, it feels less personal. Make sure you know every name perfectly right from the start.

7. Conduct

How do you engage all participants in your session?

Conducting is the social side of facilitation. Whenever I facilitate a group of people, I can predict the quality of the output by the quality of their conversations. The quality of conversation is a direct consequence of the coherence of the group. It is a consequence of the alignment of each participant to a common purpose and their level of trust in each other and their collaborative potential. Trust is a prerequisite for people to open up and connect with each other in honest conversation.

So, trust enables quality conversations, but what makes the content of conversations worthwhile? I am not sure which wise person said it first, but *energy flows where attention goes*. When something gets your attention it often 'grows' or becomes a bigger part of your life. When you have the intention to buy a new car, and you are interested in a certain type of car or a brand, suddenly you will see it everywhere on the road.

Another example of this principle: say nice words every day to one plant in your house and deliberately ignore another. After a while you will see the difference in their growth: the plant you spoke to so nicely will have grown more than the one you ignored. This is the same principle as the 'Heart hugs' I described to you in Chapter 5. If you direct your attention to someone with positive emotions, you foster connection with your energy.

For some reason, we have eyes to see colors and shapes, we have ears to register sound, tastebuds to enjoy taste, but we do not have such an amazing mechanism to experience energy. We can sense it without having a specific 'sense' designed for it. We often feel different when a certain person enters the room, or when someone gets really angry without saying anything.

I have witnessed huge differences in the quality of conversations and interpretations when people direct their attention and energy completely to the conversation. When they really pay attention to each other and to specific topics, together, it often yields insightful conclusions. But unfortunately, it seems we all have an attention deficit disorder from time to time.

Focusing your attention and energy together in the moment can lead to exciting conversations. It even promotes the production of feel-good hormones like dopamine, endorphins and anandamide. The last one actually promotes lateral thinking. It seems nature has built us in such a way that we get rewarded for focusing our energy together. On the other hand, it is exhausting to live a life where you are continuously distracted and feel as if you lack the time and the space to do anything properly with enough focus.

No wonder people get so tired of all the meetings they have to sit through. If you look at people's Outlook planners today, it looks like losing a Tetris game. They are completely filled with all these different colored blocks. A full day or full morning without meetings is very rare. The days look fragmented, jumping from one topic to the next. People have to pre-block time in their agenda so no one else can put in a meeting. A strange phenomenon when you think about it. It feels like other people can attack you with meetings at any time and you have to defend yourself by pre-blocking your time.

The social part of facilitation is about directing everyone's attention completely to the conversations. This can be quite a challenge in our current world. This practice of directing attention is called 'conducting'. And with conducting you can increase the level of engagement of all participants, connecting their heads. But before I explain to you how to do that, let me first tell you what a lack of engagement looks like.

WHAT DOES LACK OF ENGAGEMENT LOOK LIKE?

People can participate, but at the same time disengage. When people decide not to direct their full attention to the conversation, the group slowly falls apart. When that happens, the best possible outcome from this group is lost, because you will not be able to tap into its full potential. People are still participating, but they are not contributing all they can. Blending all individuals into an individual group means you leverage all the available minds to get to the best output. How? You can leverage the available minds by directing their attention.

In general, people disengage whenever they feel their efforts will not make a difference. This feeling can be caused by all kinds of things, not always within the control of the facilitator. People might hold back because of the competitiveness of the organizational culture, or they might feel threatened by hierarchy.

But there are also some typical things that you as a facilitator can control. A common situation which may cause disengagement happens when the facilitator is wearing multiple 'hats'. More often than not, topic experts are asked to facilitate meetings and workshops which create output related to their area of expertise. In most cases this will have a very profound impact on key projects in which they have already invested a lot of energy. Here, a bias is almost inevitable. This captain knows where this ship should be going and will try and influence the course in their preferred direction. How can you expect an expert not to be emotionally invested in the output when they are *the* key stakeholder of the gathering?

It is never a good idea to take part in a conversation and facilitate the conversation at the same time. As the captain, you have a lot of power. You are the owner of time, the guardian of space, you are guiding and conducting to safely get a group to shore. If you are wearing a second hat as expert and contributor, you will be unable to get the most out of your group. They will obviously know you are a topic expert, which will make them sensitive to your opinion. They will immediately feel overpowered if you share your opinion based on all your experience. There is a high risk that they will feel that their efforts will not matter that much. And even if they entered the space believing you will be a completely unbiased captain, it only takes one or two critical remarks from your side to lose all their trust. And that will kickstart their disengagement.

If you are biased, you are unconsciously influencing the output. The participants will feel they will not get the chance to fully contribute. There is no real safe space. If you are a topic expert, it would be best to get a great captain so you can completely focus on sharing your expertise without having to facilitate.

let me give you another example of disengagement setting in. People lose interest when their perspective is not taken into account. The best example is when the team decides to vote. Everyone adds one, two or three votes to their preferred choice and the team ends up with a visual representation of the consensus. How can you argue with the chosen direction when it is clearly the choice of the team that received the most votes?

By paying attention to outliers, better arguments can be built to support the final collective choice.

If the session continues at that point, the team members who did not vote for that choice, will start to disengage. They will probably still participate, but they will not feel their voice matters that much. These 'outliers' might have had great reasons for having a different opinion, but now it got lost, so they disconnect from where the team is going. Before deciding to move forward, it is important to understand who did not agree, and especially: why. Often, they agree to the same general choice, but they have some concerns or nuances that can be crucial requirements for successful deployment (at least from their point of view). By paying attention to outliers, better arguments can be built to support the final collective choice.

Whenever a decision is made in a gathering, enough time and attention need to be spent on the argumentation behind the decision. This is a very important moment of closure, and it will determine whether you can continue with the full force of the group or with only half of it. I have been part of a lot of meetings with disengaged people. Meetings that were packed with agenda points and too little time to make decisions without losing anyone in the process. A facilitator should make sure all perspectives get attention from the group when decisions are made. Everyone deserves some airtime and the full attention of the team. This will keep everyone on board.

DIRECTING ATTENTION TO INCREASE ENGAGEMENT

If the cause of disengagement lies within the control of the facilitator, it often has to do with the way a facilitator is directing the attention of the group. Some people, topics, arguments, perspectives do not get sufficient attention, resulting in subpar conversations. The best possible interpretations and results then ar not realized. A conducting facilitator directs attention to include everyone's perspective and all relevant content.

Direct attention to other participants. A lot of things can happen to keep people from paying enough attention to each other during conversation. The usual suspects are Outlook, Messenger, WhatsApp and Slack: distractions that have become a fixed part of many people's lives. It has become a habit to keep track of anything coming in through these channels, not to mention all the other social media. As it is a habit, people are unaware of the level of distraction it is causing. Especially during online sessions, it can wreak havoc on the quality of conversations. During online sessions you can easily send emails or messages without anyone noticing. Unless you forget to put yourself on mute and the typing sound from your keyboard echoes through the discussion. You would be surprised how often that happens.

But even in offline sessions people often also have a hard time putting away their phones. All these social apps are especially created to keep you hooked. That is the very reason they exist. If a marketing department wants to build an app for their customers, the first thing they think about is how frequently the customers need the content, and what the hook is to keep them coming back. Otherwise, there is no point in building an app. So, if you put your device in front of you during a session, you are basically saying: 'the content coming from my apps, or the calls I might be receiving, are important enough to make me stop listening to all of you'.

The first step in directing attention towards each other is to deal with these habits of distraction: you need to lay out some ground rules. Make sure everyone acknowledges how detrimental these distractions are to the quality of conversations. Come to an agreement on how to avoid them together. Like gathering all the phones in a box and keeping them aside until the break.

Every time I forgot to lay out the ground rules for interaction and distraction, I had a much harder time driving engagement as a facilitator. Whenever I called out the distracted people to share their thoughts on the matter, they would ask me to repeat the question. They had heard their names but were too busy with other things. When I repeated the question, their answers would be random or completely beside the point. They missed the context. This is a real disruptor to the flow of the conversation for all the other participants. The distracted participants actually became a distraction for all the others.

With ground rules in place, people might still get distracted, but these distractions will be manageable, because you as a facilitator can always refer them back to the rules you all agreed on.

Direct attention to content. Participation and engagement can be absolutely great during the session, but conversations can still derail in all directions – or even get stuck – because of a confusing or even disturbing comment.

Some of the most enjoyable sessions I have experienced were between colleagues who consider themselves friends. The atmosphere is always great, they know each other so well that they can joke about anything. No one feels threatened, and everyone is open towards each other. Idea generation sessions are usually their favorite type of gatherings. They have the best time getting creative with each other. I have the best time as well, observing their enthusiasm. But, be careful: when they start joking around too much and move away from the topics that are on the table, it is hard to reel them back in.

How do you get them back on track? It is tricky, because you do not want to become the party pooper. The rules of thumb for giving instructions apply. It needs to be short, with the right words and the right tone of voice, remember? You want to keep the wind in the sails as you are changing the course of the ship.

At times, your goal is to steer participants into the right direction again. Especially during divergent activities, like brainstorming, when you want them to have broad conversations and see possibilities but not go off track. At other times, you want the group to come to a conclusion together. Especially in convergent activities, when you need them to agree and make a choice. The latter can be a bit harder because it may end a very enjoyable or lively conversation. In both cases, the facilitator's goal is to keep building on the energy level. The way you direct their attention can leverage the momentum, but it can also cut into their flow.

THE STORY FUELS THE PURPOSE

I have been part of sessions where good conversations suddenly came to a standstill, and energy dropped. I remember a session where I had a group sharing their experiences related to the COVID pandemic. It was an 'empathy check-in' to kickstart a session on solving loneliness during COVID times. One of the participants shared a story about a person, she knew quite well, who took their own life during COVID. It caught everyone by surprise and naturally everyone expressed their sympathy. Then, everybody became very quiet and felt a bit shocked. There was a lot of empathy for sure. All participants understood the seriousness of the challenge we were to solve in our gathering.

But it was hard to move forward after this shock. It felt awkward to say anything to bring the conversation to another topic. And so, no one dared to say anything. This is a typical moment where the facilitator's conducting skills can re-infuse the conversation with energy and kickstart the necessary momentum. The trick here is to build on this story to get everyone back on track. You cannot ignore, dismiss or pay insufficient attention to sensitive and personal shared content. The facilitator needs to point out the value of this story to reach the overall goal, to find solutions for loneliness. At that moment I asked: 'Well, what can we learn from this story, what should we take along on our mission to find ways to help these people who suffer so much from loneliness?' I had everyone share their take-away from the story in the light of the overall goal. The power of the story was used to fuel the purpose of the gathering, and it gave everyone energy and meaning to the process of finding solutions.

Another situation where conversation came to a complete standstill happened when I asked someone from the group to moderate a sharing round with all participants. I sometimes do this when I feel that the team does not take enough ownership of the gathering. This time, I asked someone to gather everyone's feedback on an outcome of an exercise. To my surprise, the person facilitating started by sharing her own opinion first. So, I waited for her to ask for someone else's point of view, but she just kept elaborating. It took a while before I finally understood that she did not have the intention to invite anyone else to speak. She took advantage of the opportunity to convince all the other participants that her opinion was the right one.

This is a valuable lesson about not just passing on facilitation tasks to anyone! The energy dropped. Some people even felt a bit annoyed at having this opinion imposed on them. I had to defuse the situation immediately. I did not want to let her continue, but I did not want to put her on the spot either. I wanted everyone, including her, to stay engaged and energized. So, I told her: 'You have provided great context for your thoughts, which helps us to understand completely where you are coming from. To make sure everyone can build on this, what do you see as the one essential opportunity for the others to take into account when

While guiding for full participation is about building trust, conducting for full engagement is about directing energy and attention.

giving their opinion?' Yes, you guessed it! I had a 'Bruce Lee' sound in my head. I did not block her, and I acknowledged her contribution. But I also helped her to make it actionable for the others to build on. She was sure that her message came across. And on the other hand, I made it easy for the next person to agree or disagree, using the 'essential point'. That made her elaborate explanation of her opinion less imposing.

Directing the attention and managing the energy in conversation are key skills to improve the output of a gathering. Let's dive deep into some conducting practices that can help you excel at captaineering.

There are four conducting practices. These will help you to direct the attention of participants to each other or to specific topics. I learned them from experience. As they are not the only ways to direct the attention of participants, keep your captain's log at hand while reading, and also while experimenting during your facilitation efforts. Feel free to explore them and to shape them further.

1. **Playing with numbers:** A conversation that happens plenary in a large group has a different dynamic than conversations in smaller groups. I refer to 'grouping' as the act of changing the size of the group for the benefit of the conversation.

2. **Playing with pace:** Another way to direct attention to the conversation with others, is by changing the rhythm of the conversation. People have to take time to lean in or save time by cutting to the chase.

3. **Keys to unlock conversations:** If I want to direct the attention towards a different perspective or a blind spot, I will nudge the group with a provocative trigger question.

4. **Orchestrate a beautiful symphony:** When someone makes
   a breakthrough comment, it needs enough attention to leverage
   it needs enough attention to leverage and build on it. Directing
   attention to specific statements and opinions is what I call
   'orchestration'.

Grouping, pacing, triggering and orchestration increase the quality of
the conversations and fuel them with energy. But how do you put them
into practice? Let's examine these practices in more detail.

1. Playing with numbers

The quality of conversations improves when the participants are prepared.
This will make them feel more confident and at ease. They are also more
eager to talk because they want to share what they have prepared. And
they are more likely to listen if they are listened to. So, I almost never
start up a conversation without giving everyone a bit of solo time. This
allows for equal participation, because everyone has their thoughts ready
to share, even the more introverted people. If I ask the group to immediately start sharing, the ones who have their ideas ready will get the most
attention. Often, these are also the people with the strongest opinions.
It will cause disengagement among the people who are not so sure yet.
Giving everyone a quiet moment to think about what they want to say
provides a comfortable start for any conversation.

SMALLER SUBGROUPS

Sometimes it may seem that jumping from solo to a group conversation is too much of a spotlight to share first thoughts. At least to some
participants. In that case, I first have them share their thoughts in smaller subgroups to get aligned with a smaller amount of people. It feels
less threatening, and it gives the participant some back-up when sharing
thoughts in a larger group. If it is a very sensitive topic, or if it is just the
early start of a session, when people are still getting to know each other,
it is a good idea to start conversations in pairs. The alignment with one
'buddy' is far less threatening, and it is a very comfortable build-up to the
group conversation.

1-2-4-ALL

This is a very popular sequence of conversational group dynamics. Everyone first starts by gathering their thoughts individually. Then they share their thoughts in pairs. The pairs merge into groups of four, and eventually all move into a plenary group. By the time everyone shares in the group, a lot of the interpretations and consolidations have already been made. For difficult topics that need a lot of argumentation this really works like a charm. As you are moving from smaller to larger groups, the argumentation behind decisions gets built. Everyone can then share solid points in the group with a lot of aligned thinking behind them.

FROM LARGE TO SMALL

It also works the other way around. When I notice that a group conversation is dominated by one or a few people with strong opinions, or when a group conversation hits a dead end, I often split them up into smaller groups or have everyone jump into solo work. Sometimes I mistakenly assume everyone is ready to start sharing their thoughts but when I give them the floor, there is only silence: no one seems to feel ready to share yet. In that case I give them more time. If I would force the group to continue having the conversation without having their thoughts ready, it could cause disengagement. Only a few will talk a lot, and the others get 'sofa syndrome', completely handing the stage over to the talkative ones. They were not ready and now have a hard time adding any new thoughts while listening.

Grouping does not always mean literally splitting up or merging smaller groups. It can also mean you bring the attention back to the group. Consider the following case. Sometimes when a participant wants to add power to their statement, they address the facilitator. This participant is looking for the most trusted person to reinforce their point and convince the group. Participants often address me when trying to make their point. The kind of 'grouping' I apply here is breaking the conversation back open to the group. I direct the attention away from myself to have the statement considered by the group. I do not express any opinion on the statement, but I immediately break the topic open to the group with questions like: 'Does everyone feel this way? Would anyone like to nuance this statement?'

Even when participants are not trying to reinforce their point, they might still address the facilitator when sharing their thoughts, simply because the facilitator is asking them to share. When someone is speaking directly to the facilitator when sharing, some of the other participants will start paying less attention and slowly disengage. The energy in the conversation will decrease. In an offline world, I would get out of the line of sight so that this person cannot look at me while sharing. They will have to look at the other participants. In an online environment, I break it open each time by calling out other people to respond. When sharing after solo work, the goal is always for the team to listen and respond to each other in order to have an in-depth conversation. The facilitator might need to direct their attention again and again towards each other when they share, so as to direct the attention away from themselves.

DIFFICULT PEOPLE: HOW DO YOU DEAL WITH THEM?

One of the questions I get most frequently in facilitation courses, is about how to deal with difficult participants. Overly critical participants can question every part of your narrative and hijack the session. By doing so, they are drawing all the attention to themselves and the energy of the conversation drops. As a facilitator you need to minimize the influence of this person to avoid disengagement among the others. When I have someone in a workshop who continuously takes the stage to express their opinion strongly – and they might be spreading some negativity – I break it open to the group consistently. Breaking it open means you ask the entire group to comment on this opinion. Usually, when the group has indicated they do not support the opinion, that person tends to become less loud and imposing. They often blend in and understand that they are expected to listen to the others as much as speak. When the loud person does get support, you can address their opinion or suggestions as a collective and adapt the program together, thus blending this person into the group again. Breaking it open for the collective mind, involving everyone to respond, can restore balance easily and allows for more coherence in the group.

Breaking it open can restore balance easily and allows for more coherence in the group.

If breaking it open does not help to minimize the influence of an overly critical participant, breaking out might do the trick. If the group breaks out into smaller teams, the critical comments are only affecting a smaller part of the team. The other sub-teams can productively collaborate to form their conclusions without the disruptive comments. You need to choose carefully who to allocate to the smaller group with the critical participant and you can decide to spend a bit more time facilitating this smaller team separately. When the conversations are more difficult because of an overly critical participant, it is easier to find common ground in a smaller group.

2. Playing with pace

Pacing the conversation means to determine the rhythm or the speed of the conversation. Sometimes it is very beneficial to slow down and allow for some time to understand each other better. Sometimes you need to pick up the pace towards the conclusion. Pace for space or pace for a race!

Without a facilitator, conversations rarely have the right pace at the right moment. When you are taking part in a conversation it is not always easy to see that a slower pace might help to create sufficient space for everyone. On the other hand, when getting to a conclusion, people have been analyzing a topic so intensely that they cannot stop explaining their interpretations. They are just repeating and reconfirming what has already been said, only in different words. They do not even realize that the conversation is going round in circles and that the time has come to race towards the finish. Time for the facilitator to step in.

Your voice is your greatest asset. As a facilitator, you have the luxury to observe conversations from the sideline, easily detecting patterns and misalignment. If you are not part of conversation and you do not have to make your point, you have more headspace to interpret what is being said. This is the best position to conduct for engagement by pacing the conversation. Determining a faster or slower rhythm, thus adding some variety to the conversation, keeps everyone engaged. Slowing down and speeding up adds a flavor of suspense and excitement to the conversation.

When determining pace, your voice is your greatest asset. For example, when I give instruction, I lower the pace. This means I speak in a lower voice, I talk a bit slower, taking my time to explain and emphasize a few words and phrases. That way everyone gets the chance to follow what I am saying and process what I mean at the same time. It is important that everyone pays close attention to anything that I say, otherwise I have to repeat instructions, which is like a slow start after the gunshot went off.

In that same way, slowing down makes sense when a conversation arrives at a milestone moment. For example, an important realization occurs, or a very difficult contradiction is puzzling everyone. A breakthrough moment is about to happen. Everyone's close attention is needed to discuss, process and make it happen. When the pace slows down, everyone in the group is able to follow the thought process and contribute. When I notice that a milestone moment is approaching, I might say something like 'let's pause for just a moment here. Paul mentioned that everyone likes ice cream.' (silence) 'But then Miguel mentioned that no one wants cows to be milked.' (silence) 'Miguel, could you remind everyone what the most significant objections against milking cows were and how people felt about them?' Then I closely observe what is being said and where I can help to connect the dots.

From the moment I say 'let's pause …', my speech has slowed down but is still firm. In an offline world, I clearly raise my hand so that everyone can see my body language supporting my intention to hit the pause button. I check everyone's attention quickly and maybe call out people who are distracted, for example: 'Marie, are you with us? this might be a key element to discuss.' I use my voice to create suspense, as if something big is going to happen, and they are all part of it.

While observing the continued conversation afterwards, I sometimes intervene again shortly when I feel I need to lower the pace. I might call out someone to also contribute, but I will use the softer voice and a bit of silence, for example 'Can I ask? (silence) … is everyone following this conversation?' (silence) 'Jennifer … what's your take on it?' This may sound a bit exaggerated, so if you apply it yourself, make sure it feels natural. If you hear more than one needle drop during your silence, you are stretching it too long. People might become bored and disengage.

Lowering the pace may feel counterintuitive when you are tight on time. But it can actually save you time. If the moment of lowering the pace results in a breakthrough conclusion or insight, the rest of the conversation will run more smoothly. The participants can build further on this insight. This breakthrough can give that necessary spark to get to an aligned conclusion. If you did not allow for the group to take a moment to dig a bit deeper, they might have never reached a meaningful conclusion together.

MOVE THEM ALONG WITH YOUR VOICE

When a group of people is arriving at a conclusion, I often notice that they start beating around the bush. Sometimes the decision has already been made, or the conclusion has already been mentioned a couple of times, but they just cannot get to a closure. They are enjoying this moment of clarity and alignment so much that they want to linger a bit. When that happens, I will pick up the pace using the necessary enthusiasm. My tone of voice will give the group a feeling of excitement. It will feel like we are moving towards closure, we are finishing an important step in our get-together. I will use words like: 'It feels like we're agreeing on an important point here. This will surely help us move forward with finding the best solution. Miguel, you just mentioned that people will be okay with milking cows if they are well taken care of. Would you mind summarizing what we have been discussing these last minutes, in just a couple of points?' When I use a higher-pitched voice and speed up the pace, with a bit of luck, Miguel will probably copy my pace and sum up everything efficiently. Without having to say it out loud, everyone will get the feeling that they are moving towards the end of discussing this topic.

If you have gained enough trust as a guide, people will often mimic you. This is the mirroring effect. When you start talking slowly and with a deeper voice, people tend to talk a bit slower as well. This form of pacing often works well together with the next two conducting practices: using provocative trigger questions and orchestrating the conversation.

3. Trigger questions are the keys to unlock conversations

Grouping and pacing are practices that direct the attention of the participants towards each other during conversation. When everyone is paying enough attention to deeply listen to each other, it might still be necessary to unlock new perspectives on the topic. To feed the conversation, the facilitator can direct attention towards some contradictions, ambiguities, blind spots or specific goals. Asking the right questions at the right time can be very powerful. It will give the quality of the conversation a boost. This power needs to be handled with care and clear intention.

Gathering your own thoughts, understanding someone else's thoughts and forming what has been said into new thoughts, are three processes that do not always happen smoothly. You need to abandon your own thoughts to have enough attention to really understand what someone else is saying. Then you need to recall what you were thinking before to connect it to this new information. These processes can run really fast and simultaneously, but it can also be a bumpy ride. People usually do not have a hard time coming up with their opinion about something. But building on each other's points, and synthesizing the different opinions while conversing, can be a hard thing to do. A facilitator can help to filter information and synthesize it towards new thoughts and conclusions by directing the attention with trigger questions. I fire off trigger questions when I notice that a conversation needs to be unlocked and pushed into a certain direction.

So, trigger questions are questions that trigger new thoughts amongst the participants. For example: 'Does this happen all the time, or only at specific occasions? And what occasions?' You are directing the attention to unlock the conversation further. Your trigger questions always have a clear intention. You are intuitively throwing in another ingredient into the conversational potion while closely monitoring the effect, but without forcing or controlling it.

KEEP IT OPEN AND RELEVANT

A good trigger question has two important characteristics. For one, it is always an open question. A facilitator should never suggest any interpretations, conclusions or decisions. The questions should help the participants to broaden their thinking. Otherwise, it will end the conversation instead of fueling it. And there will be a risk of disengagement and a drop in energy in case your implied answers are not accepted by everyone.

The second key characteristic is: relevance. The trigger question should be spontaneous. The best trigger questions are usually not prepared. They pop up intuitively, when the facilitator has an open focus. Experience does help. But when if you are stressed into a narrow focus, the right triggers will not pop up from your memory. Remember open and narrow focus from Chapter 4? You can be creative and have the perfect trigger questions popping up, out of the blue, when you maintain an open focus during the conversation. This means you cannot judge what is being said, and you should not get carried away by your own opinions or emotions about the topic. You need to be able to park your own personality for a while and take on a 'generative' mode. A generative mode is an openness that allows you to see all possible opportunities without any preferences or blind spots. In Part 3, I will explain how you can nurture such a state.

Although trigger questions are best when they are spontaneous, you can re-use certain trigger questions. You may just want to tweak the wording to make it as impactful and relevant as possible in the moment. The more you try to come up with great questions, and monitor their impact on the conversation, the better you get at being a questioner or a 'trigger'. So, every time you notice that your trigger questions worked like a charm to unlock the conversation, write them down in your captain's log and add a description of their effect.

These are some examples of trigger questions that have served my captaineering well.

'What would our typical employee have to say about this? In their words?'
'Did this point come up before? And when, in what context?'
'How does this serve the goal or purpose of our meeting?'
'What aspects should we definitely take along in our further conversation? What did we learn from this?'
'So, what motivates and what demotivates to behave in the desired way?'
'When does this happen? What are the moments of truth when this really comes to play?'
'What part of this is actionable, and what part is not?'
'Which difficulties are contextual, and which ones are permanent?'
'How does this connect to any of our conclusions before?'
'What changes everything? What is totally different from our first thinking?'

The inspiration for a trigger question should only be the spur of the conversational moment. There should not be any standards for these questions, as they might limit the spontaneity. But I can point out certain directions to help you on your way. Looking at the questions before, you will see that they have a couple of different intentions.

- They bring in either time or a different perspective.
- They connect to previous conversations or conclusions.
- They connect back to goals to conclude and move forward.
- They trigger empathy to see through someone else's eyes.

Let me simplify this even more: you can be aiming for more context, for empathy, for different angles (to explore or even disrupt), for contradictions or for key learnings. The latter I often use to create a feeling of progress in the conversation. I trigger the participants to narrow the conversation down to the most valuable insights we should take along in the light of our goals. A sense of progress helps to highlight the meaning behind the conversation, and fuels engagement again.

To help you to become a pro at trigger questions, I have three more tips that will enhance your triggering practice.

Never be afraid to use triggers. When a conversation stays stuck for too long, if it goes in circles or becomes silent, energy will drop and people will disengage. It always takes some effort to get them back into the flow, and it becomes harder each time. Throw in timely trigger questions to keep momentum going.

Timing is key. Asking too many trigger questions can overwhelm the group and confuse them. They need to get the chance to work through the first trigger question before you launch the next one. If it goes too quickly, the power of the first question might get lost. But if you sense that your trigger question had an undesired effect on the conversation, you should immediately rephrase it or replace it with another one.

Language increases the impact of the trigger. Ask the participants to share their thoughts in the words of the customer, the hotel guest, the consumer, etc. Ask them to try to articulate their thoughts using specific language and even quotes, especially when you are triggering for different perspectives. Using the language, the type of words, that a specific person would use,

Using the language that a specific person would use, will help everyone to empathize more.

will help everyone to empathize more with the perspective of that person.

Trigger questions are a powerful tool. They provide more structure to conversations. They can reinforce the trust in you as a facilitator, but they can also decrease the trust if the questions are overwhelming, closed or leading. It is best to experiment a lot and pay close attention to the reactions to your trigger questions.

Before we jump into the final conducting practice of orchestrating – one of my favorites – let's recap the previous practices. *Grouping* and *pacing* will direct everyone's attention to each other, in conversation. *Trigger questions* will then direct attention to blind spots, different perspectives or goals, triggering thought processes that fuel the conversation.

4. Orchestrating conversation

Once the conversation has gained momentum, the quality depends on the amount and the kind of connections that are made between the different shared thoughts. To what extent is everyone building on each other's contributions, instead of just sharing them? Even when listening deeply to each other, somehow the interplay of shared thoughts does not organically lead to the necessary conclusions. It is like an orchestra where everyone is playing their instrument, but they cannot seem to align into a symphony. The facilitator can orchestrate this alignment by directing their attention to the sound of the other instruments. We do not just want to make all kinds of sounds; we want to make music together.

When individual opinions are shared in a group, it often leads to contradictions, ambiguity and confusion. Some facilitators tend to shy away from potential difficult discussion, because it might harm the safe space. People might want to disengage and even disconnect when discussions become heated. But the best conclusions are often born out of controversy. By avoiding controversy, you might end up with superficial insights or solutions. They key is to leverage the trust and conduct the energy during conversation in order to align the instruments. There is harmony to be found in hard rock!

We do not just want to make all kinds of sounds; we want to make music together.

HOW TO BECOME THE CONDUCTOR OF YOUR ORCHESTRA

How do you orchestrate? When I notice that everyone is engaged in conversation, but they are not yet seeing the potential of some points shared by a participant, I will direct their attention to these points. I am not just repeating the point someone has made. First, I hit the pause button and catch everyone's attention, using my voice to lower the pace. I am cutting into the flow of the conversation. This can be disruptive, so I need to be sure that the point has a lot of potential of increasing the conversation quality. Secondly, when I have everyone's attention, I ask the person to repeat the point, but with some context as to why it needs more attention. It could be that this shared point is contradictory to a statement made earlier by someone else. Or it could be a completely surprising new insight, or a great expansion of a point made before. Whatever the case, a facilitator's intention is to rewire the conversation for a more effective build-up to the best possible shared understanding.

When you pay close attention as a facilitator, you can see where the conversation is going. You also notice when people are making the same point more often, which might pull the conversation in a similar direction over and over. You can also see when there is a lack of depth in understanding each other's thoughts. When no thoughts with great potential have yet been shared, you can use a trigger question. But when someone already said something that might trigger an important thought process, it is much more effective to use the point that person made.

When you are using a previously shared thought, by having the participant repeat it, you are building on the momentum of the conversation, energizing and fueling it. This is different from using trigger questions. When firing off a trigger question, people still need time to think about it, and it can be more of a reboot than a boost for the conversation. In other words, trigger questions unlock while orchestration tunes.

With orchestration, you also risk decreasing the momentum of the conversation. When you bring up a point again that causes controversy, it might cause friction between participants. Therefore, it is crucial to provide the necessary context of why it makes sense to spend more time and attention to a controversial point that has been made. This means you have to point out the value of considering the controversial point.

Let me show you an example. Rick has been working on a project for a year to make more data readily available in the Customer Relationship Management (CRM) system. Paula just mentioned that their client survey pointed out that the data their clients really need is not provided in Rick's CRM system upgrade. Paula makes the point, but the conversation continues without enough attention to it. Bringing up Paula's point again might wreak havoc on the conversation and cause some seriously heated discussions. But it also brings up an important point of view from the client side. If I would ask Paula just to repeat the point she made, I am not really embedding it well into the ongoing conversation. I want to make sure that the conversational momentum is maintained, so I need to point out the value of Paula's point for the conversation and its participants.

As a facilitator, I could say: 'Paula just brought up the research that provided insight into the kind of information that clients need. Our intention is to build something great for these customers. But we don't have them sitting here at the table to tell us what they want. It might be good to have a listen again to what Paula knows about the customer's wants and needs from that research. Can we please hear the highlights again, Paula? Let's cross-check what confirms and what contradicts the things we know.'

A facilitator is not home free by just embedding a controversial point back into the conversation, but it is a start. When you are moving towards some controversy, it helps to keep repeating the value of certain content for the discussion. And it often helps to break things open to the group and involve the collective mind to answer the why's behind contradiction and ambiguity. Usually, when controversy happens, only a few participants become very active in conversation, the ones who are most emotionally invested in the discussion. This has a polarizing effect on the conversation. A facilitator can avoid a drop in energy by balancing the conversation and move towards consensus by involving all perspectives around the table.

Although sensitive topics can seem daunting to a facilitator, these are the biggest opportunities to achieve a breakthrough. Look at it this way: Rick probably already knew about the research that Paula was referring to. It might even be an unexpressed frustration for him. The triggers for controversy in conversation are often things that should be worked through to get to a breakthrough and better collaboration. But when it is sensitive, these things can start having a life of their own below the surface. A good facilitator can work with trust and energy to have a great empathic sharing moment on sensitive topics. They can lead the difficult conversation towards a constructive conclusion while making sure all parties see the value in the 'closure' moment. Facilitators make sure no one is left out of the consensus. That is their job.

In other words, if a facilitator avoids controversial conversations, they rob the group of their breakthrough moment. It is like aligning the instruments but only if they all sound like a trumpet. You will never end up with a beautiful symphony. A double bass might sound gloomy, while a violin can sound a bit more cheerful, if you combine them with a cello it becomes a feast for the ears.

Now that you are already familiar with trigger questions, let's get you on your way with orchestration as well. Here are four tips for creating wonderful symphonies.

Timing is always key. If you feel the conversation is already on the verge of becoming a heated discussion, do not add fuel to the fire. Important points that might result into a breakthrough moment should never be ignored. But directing attention to them will have most impact when the energy is still good and everyone feels they are making progress. The point was brought up a while ago, you just need to make it relevant again. You need to position it back into the conversation. It is important to remember that you do not necessarily have to emphasize something when it has just been said. You can wait for a better moment if that allows you to embed it into the conversation more effectively.

Orchestration is about inclusiveness. When you know everyone's background, you can call out people who have an expert opinion. Even when there is no particular expert in the room, leveraging diversity will always lead to higher-quality conversations. Calling out people to respond to

This is when facilitation becomes similar to surfing the waves and reading the sea for the best waves.

what others have just shared renders some variety to the conversation and helps to trigger imagination. As I already mentioned in the previous chapter, use first names so people feel more involved and will share more of their thoughts.

Orchestration navigates through controversy. When people disagree, it serves as a great opportunity to reach new conclusions. If they agree, they already understand each other's viewpoints. If they disagree, there are arguments to 'mine' in the conversation. That is what orchestrating through controversy means. It is a practice of surfacing valuable arguments that underpin different viewpoints. By directing everyone's attention to these arguments, it will lead to new insights and conclusions. Facilitators often shy away from controversy because there is a risk of derailment. But this is when facilitation becomes similar to surfing the waves and reading the sea for the best waves. It is the most exciting part. If you don't drown.

Consensus is not the goal. This is such an important point that I need to spend a bit more time explaining it. Consensus is *never* the primary goal. By consensus, I mean that everyone agrees with a consolidated output. Bringing to the surface important opinions, considering other perspectives, interpreting perspectives with empathy: these are the primary goals of conversations. If in the end participants agree to disagree, there can be value in that as well. In this case, important opposing arguments still stand, even after a lively conversation. When that happens, I will ask the participants to help me understand how we can build on the arguments.

The reason why facilitators often feel the rush to arrive at consensus is because they think they need to make sure that the answers are provided in the end. They feel it is their responsibility to ensure consolidation. But it is not. It is the facilitator's responsibility to get the most out of the team by increasing coherence. Sometimes participants understand each other deeply but still disagree. Compromising should not be forced but facilitated. Maybe compromises can more easily be found in a next step or another activity. You cannot force growth, you can only nurture growth.

It should be clear by now that a facilitator should never aim only for consensus at the end of an activity. With the following example I will show you how a next step can offer resolution, even without consolidation at the end of the previous step.

Imagine a team needs to decide which is the best solution from all the possible solutions that came out of their brainstorm. When discussing all the criteria and arguments, they just cannot seem to agree on the best one. The conversation gets stuck over and over in all the details of feasibility, viability and even potential technical features. The group's vision gets blurred by all the talking, and they lose track of the essential benefits of each solution from the user's point of view.

You cannot force growth, you can only nurture growth.

STAGES	① UNPACKING	② EXPLORING	③ USING	④ STORING
TASKS	• Open packaging • Organise all elements • Separate cardboard from plastic • Identify/find the on- or offline manual	• Read manual • Search 'How-to's' on YouTube • Assemble product	• Prep the product • Use the product • See the result	• Disassemble for storage • Store all elements
KEY CHALLENGES	• Too much plastic • Too many booklets → Need for a more simple experience	• Too much to read • Complicated assembly → Need to start using immediately	• Hard to find the 'on' button • Confusing how to increase power → Need for plug 'n play easy interface	• A lot of small pieces to store → Need for compact storing
SOLUTIONS	• Minimise plastic • Include guide → How to fold cardboard	Product is already assembled → Guide how to disassemble		All small pieces can be stored inside the product
BENEFITS	End result: Small volume of folded cardboard	End result: Ready for use with visible 'on' button + fully charged battery		End result: Only two larger components to be stored

Fig. 3 This is just one example of how you can merge several options into one 'closure summary'. All the options/solutions are combined within the user's experience (the broader picture). If the team can't decide on one option, make sure the broader picture combining several options makes sense to them as a starting point for the next step.

At this stage, there is no point in forcing the team to decide and consolidate on one or two solutions. They need more structural thought processes to work their way through it. It could help to have them select a number of solutions and structurally describe the benefits and potential of each. In a next step, they could then start connecting these ideas, knowing the benefits and potential of each solution. Then they could define this concept solution as an aggregation of the ideas described earlier. In a next step, they could start building a future scenario from the user's perspective. At each stage, the team can point out the benefit of any of the sub-ideas provided at any stage of the user's experiences. See Fig. 3 on the previous page.

This consolidation was not about having the team decide on one or two ideas when they were not ready, just to finish the brainstorm with one consolidated idea. The consolidation was about defining the new reality of a user when experiencing a new approach, consisting of maybe a couple of smaller ideas. This consolidation happened at a later stage.

You see? As a facilitator, you should never have a preconceived notion of what the exact output of a step should be. It is what makes most sense to the team and serves the team at that point in time. This might even mean that the output contains some pros and cons, and closure is about making sure they are all captured, and that everyone feels comfortable about building on them in a next step.

PREPARE FOR SUCCESS

Now, get ready for some practical advice on how to prepare for successful conducting.

Let me show you some practical ways to prepare for full engagement. There are three important elements here:

1. knowing who is participating;
2. thinking about the rules for interaction, and;
3. taking in account any conventions and policies.

With a great team and solid ground rules, it then makes sense to avoid as many distractions as possible by spending some time on practicalities like the size of the room and the set-up, or the access to and user-friendliness of online collaboration tools.

AN ENERGISING CONDUCTOR

Once you have gained enough trust, you can direct the attention of participants towards controversial topics and ideas. A high level of engagement will then lead to some great insights and decisions, fueling the gathering with energy. Conducting conversations is all about conducting the energy in the room, directing attention towards breakthroughs.

But that does not mean that there will be enough ownership by the team. It is one thing to be willing to share thoughts and build upon the thoughts of others, it is quite another thing to really commit to the purpose and the team. Getting full commitment needs catalysing, on top of conducting and guiding. What is catalysing, you wonder? I will explain it to you in the next chapter.

Stay the course. You can't discover a new land without first losing sight of the shore. The greatest adventure is what lies ahead.

Leverage team diversity

Not having a team ready at the start of the process provides you with the luxury of composing the right team that fits the purpose of the session. When you already have a core team, you can decide to add more out-side-in perspective, 'voice-of-the-customer', or 'flavor' by inviting extra participants. Diversity, along with the amount of people, are the two variables to work with.

Why is diversity so important? Well, because the best output comes from a melting pot of different perspectives, styles and personalities. When you have a core team that has already been working together for a long time, every individual has grown collaborative habits. They know each other well, and they trigger the same kind of behavior and thinking in each other. It is like that once-a-month Friday team meeting you have been having for years, with similar agendas and 'sharing rounds'. Each and every time the usual suspects show critical behavior, and the others show the same disengagement. This type of meetings does not really generate any surprising new perspectives or approaches. Often, they just trigger similar thinking and conclusions. This is when your 'safe space' turns from a 'brave space' into a 'cave space', disconnected from influences from the outside world. But when you bring in people from other departments or from outside the organization, a different conversational dynamic occurs. The usual suspects do not play the same roles anymore. Diversity breaks with habitual thinking and routine behavior. It will set you up for interesting conversation.

When evaluating the level of diversity in the team I will be working with, I always make use of four pillars.

Diversity of expertise. What are the different skillsets across the participants? Do they have a different track record, different work experiences, did they study different things, and do they have different certifications? Have they been working in different domains within the organization? Some expertise is necessary to serve as a solid foundation and a soundboard. Other expertise is necessary to challenge the conventional thinking.

Sometimes the most relevant expertise comes from the most unexpected corners. For example, Google has been hiring people with a hospitality background because these people have very service-oriented mindsets. Google's core business is not hospitality, but people from hospitality can bring in the necessary expertise.

Diversity of personality. If I can figure out whether I have more analytical people in the session – people looking for a lot of structure and methods – I can make sure to balance it out with more artistic and creative people. A good balance between both is important, because you need participants who can easily open up to new perspectives, and you need participants who can bring structure and provide conclusions. Another reason you need both is because they can help each other to come out of their comfort zone.

I have facilitated meetings with almost only analytical participants. They were already convinced of the best output at the start of the meeting. They just needed everyone else to get on their wagon. This can lead to very exhausting one-sided discussions. Similarly, I have facilitated creative meetings with mostly creative thinkers. They would derail from the first minute. I would be reeling them back in, again and again and again, until they accused me of being a very narrow-minded facilitator (ouch!).

To make the equation more complicated, I met very outspoken, extroverted, analytical and creative thinkers, and more introverted ones. Before a workshop you do not know whether a participant is more extroverted or introverted. Therefore, I recommend making an analysis of the invited team together with one or two key stakeholders or project owner who know the participants. It helps if someone can give you some descriptions of the different invited personalities in order to prepare.

Another approach is to have 15-minute informal phone calls with a handful of participants before the session. Having a short conversation to get to know each other, and to check expectations, will help you to understand their expertise and personality better. The tone of voice, their choice of words and the underlying emotions speak volumes. Plan these calls at quiet moments when you are available to listen deeply.

Diversity of background. Where do participants live? What kind of culture are they from? If you facilitate gatherings with people from over the world, considering the different cultures and customs is crucial for success. Tone of voice, words and expressions are not interpreted in the same way everywhere. For example, when conducting for controversy, you need to take into account that not all cultures deal with confrontation in the same way. In Dutch culture it is normal to say what is on your mind, and it is okay if you put it out there bluntly. They just like to be clear about things. In general, Western Europeans and North Americans deal well with direct confrontation. East Asians tend to perceive direct confrontation as unnecessary and sometimes immature. They will give subtle cues to their disagreement. They draw attention to concerns more subtly, using stories and metaphors, and soft descriptions of foreseen difficulties. Direct disagreement might damage the harmony and even the working relationship.

As a facilitator in cross-cultural sessions, you need to feel when to tone down or tune up the differences in opinions. A loss of face for certain cultures can mean disengagement and disconnection, with a loss of trust in the facilitator and the session. As part of your preparation as a facilitator, it is worth it to check whether there are any significant cultural differences. Also: think about how you can use any cultural differences to the session's advantage. Participants with different backgrounds can help shed a new light on behavior or emotions. These perspectives can be very relevant, especially if the session has a social purpose, for example 'improving the social experience for expats in a foreign country'.

The right number of people

What is the best number of people to facilitate? To keep everyone engaged in quality conversation, five to six people is the optimum number of participants per facilitator. From seven or more, it becomes a lot harder to keep everyone closely involved in the moment. 'Sofa syndrome' can rear its ugly head. Participants can easily think that the others will provide enough brainpower to get to the right output, and that their input is not a necessity. Distractions like email will lure them out of the conversational momentum.

With less than five participants, especially when it gets down to three, there is not enough diversity. You will notice that the conversations end quickly. There are not enough different takes on the topic, and the few viewpoints that are brought to the table are not really challenged. Building on that point, if you have six participants, but some are very alike in their thinking and opinions, you actually have less than six participants. So make sure that when you take in account the number of participants, evaluate the diversity first. That way you can be sure that each participant contributes a different perspective.

When facilitating a meeting or workshop with twenty to thirty people by yourself, there is no chance of having a quality in-depth conversation. You are rather hosting a series of presentations or a webinar, potentially with Q&A's. There is no chance of conducting conversations properly between that many people. Attempting to create conversations with a large group of people and only a few facilitators will lead to superficial interpretations and conventional conclusions or solutions. You can solve this by adding more facilitators to achieve a ratio of one facilitator per five participants.

Ground rules for interaction

An easy way to prepare for conducting is setting some ground rules. They fall into two categories. On one hand, they can help to minimize the amount of distraction people can cause. Think about ensuring that participants arrive on time, come prepared, and understand their role as contributor and the role of the facilitator. It can also be distracting in conversation when participants disagree without providing proper arguments. To smoothen the conversation, I add a ground rule called 'walk the talk', agreeing together that it is always up to the 'challenger' to provide a clear 'why' to their opinion. The reason why is often more important to the depth of the conversation than expressing the opinion.

On the other hand, it makes sense to install some ground rules that encourage interaction. Think about rules that give the participants time and space to express their opinion, that encourage deep listening and that encourage people to speak out at all times. I always remind everyone that this is 'the' moment which has been created to share thoughts. If you hold back, you will miss out. If you want to make a point, now is the time to do so. Attention to your thoughts will never be as focused as during the moment.

Ground rules to avoid distraction and to encourage interaction create the right setting to direct everyone's attention and to successfully conduct conversations. It is a good idea to share your rules in the invitation and then reinforce them at the start of any session.

Let me summarize these examples:

Ground rules to avoid distractions:
- Come prepared
- Start on time
- Walk your talk

Ground rules to encourage interaction:
- Share views and concerns and ask for feedback
- Give each other time and space
- Listen with an open mind

Practicalities

The most disruptive distractions that you cannot avoid with ground rules, are the ones caused by the set-up of the environment, online or offline. To illustrate the importance of arranging all practicalities upfront, let me share some of my past experiences or 'bloopers'.

AN ONLINE IDEATION SESSION WITH A SHARED EXCEL FILE

As a platform for ideation, this session only had an Excel file available for all participants to share their ideas in real time. As an outside facilitator, I did not even have access to the file, someone from the team had to share it in the video platform for me to see what was written by the participants. The file had colored squares to write in: the Excel version of sticky notes. Working with too many people in a shared Excel file, that needed to update real-time for everyone to see each other's ideas, is not the best set-up for ideation, to say the least. I planned the session so that we did not have to write too much, but we spent most time listening to each other via the video platform. I asked everyone to write things down on a piece of paper first, before entering ideas into the Excel file. This worked quite well in the beginning, but I made one mistake. I was naive to think that we could end the ideation with a quick brainwriting exercise in Excel. Brainwriting is an exercise where everyone picks an idea, and in a couple of rounds, everyone has to improve the idea someone else picked. It is a structured way of building on each other's ideas. By applying brainwriting in Excel, I figured I would still capture the most important ideas, and expansions on ideas. The momentum was really good by the time we reached the brainwriting exercise.

After everyone finally arrived at the right sheet and understood the instructions, two people were not able write in the 'squares'. By the fourth round two more participants could not write in the squares anymore and one participant got thrown out of the shared file. The others could not see the updated version of the file. Some had to go back to writing things on paper. The sharing of idea improvements became a real mess. Energy dropped, people disconnected and they were not pleased with the results. No one could recap any of the initial good ideas from the first ideations steps because of the confusion. I failed to prepare for how to deal with the potential technical challenges of this way of working. In the end, an additional session had to be organized to finalize the ideation.

A FULL DAY OFFLINE WORKSHOP WITH TOOLS PRINTED ON 21 A0 POSTERS

This group of people consisted of twenty participants, divided into three teams. When I arrived, several people were already sitting in the room, working at heavy wooden tables that had been placed at the center of the room. There were about eight large tables and they filled up almost the entire room. I needed one wall to project PowerPoint presentation, the other wall was decorated with some fabric that did not agree well with Tesa tape. The other two walls consisted of floor-to-ceiling windows. I asked the early birds to leave the room, and then I had to take out almost all the tables and look for some extra wall space in the hallway for two teams to work on the posters with sticky notes.

This meant I had to facilitate three teams, two of which were working outside the room with people passing by in the hallway having a chat. After lunch I had to remove even more tables because people could not move freely when we shared results plenarily. It was not the best workshop I ever facilitated. I did not make sure there was enough space for all the participants to work in. More importantly, I had planned some grouping to smoothen all conversations and ended up having smaller groups of people chatting across the complete floor of the building. It is hard to give any instructions or time indications when you cannot find half of your crew anywhere.

A MEETING WITH BREAK-OUTS FOR FIFTEEN EXECUTIVES

When I arrived for this facilitation job, I learned that the break-out rooms were small meeting rooms a bit further down the hallway, past the pantry. After breaking out into smaller teams, I could only observe and facilitate one team at a time. The distance to the other small team was too great to observe anything. So, the unobserved team would take advantage of the situation by finishing their activities and conversations quickly, and then grab a coffee at the pantry and hang out there or start working on their emails. When I managed to get one team going, the other team would have fallen apart by the time I got there. In the end I invited them to work on activities plenary to avoid any more break-outs. The continuous disengagement was impossible to manage. Had I known beforehand where the rooms were located, I would not have planned break-outs in the first place.

When I arrived, I noticed we were assigned to the smallest meeting room in the building. And it had no windows. Apparently, all other meeting rooms were booked, although the session had been scheduled two months earlier. The meeting room was just big enough for the table in the middle and a few chairs around it. People had no space to pass behind the chairs if someone was seated. Lunch was served in that same room, and I brought along some printed tools to hang on the wall, hoping for sufficient wall space.

After lunch, the room looked like a complete mess. Oxygen seemed to have decided not to stay in the room either, so I finally decided to move part of the program outside. We still had some breakthroughs by organizing talking-walks with alternating conversation partners. Instead of using the printed tools, we ended up sticking some brown paper on a wall outside. We finalized our session by sketching out some of the agreed directions on that brown paper. Although I did not book the meeting room, I learned that it is worth double-checking the room available for the workshop. If I had known about the size of the room upfront, I would have changed the program to fit in more outdoor activities.

Technical challenges, spaces that are too small for grouping or distant break-out rooms can really make it hard to keep the energy up and ensure quality conversations. You cannot visit every location beforehand, but you can make a checklist of key practical requirements when building your narrative and your team. If you need to solve practical issues on the spot, the risk of disengagement is high. It is best to prepare your virtual or real space in detail.

When listing your requirements for an offline space, take in account the room you need for grouping. If you plan to split up the group often, you need the space to maneuver.

And when listing your requirements for an online space, think about the experience invitees have with online tools. Consider a separate initiation to familiarize them with the tools beforehand. And consider a tech support to help anyone who is still struggling during the session, so as not to cause disruption.

Captain's Log

Time to try out some new conducting techniques. Don't forget to note down the effect and the challenges you take from each experiment.

Experiment 1 / START SOLO

Anytime you want your team to have a balanced conversation, allow each participant to write down their thoughts in silence first. When participants join the conversation prepared, they are more likely to share their opinion and listen to other opinions …

Always keep the solo preparation time short, followed by plenty of time to share and discuss.

A couple of minutes of solo preparation is enough to bring out the top-of-mind ideas that kickstart an in-depth conversation.

Experiment 2 / PLAY WITH YOUR VOICE

Next time you give instructions during your session, pay attention to the way you use your voice …

Start talking with a louder, more excited voice to get everyone's attention for the instructions.

During explanation of the actual tasks, talk more slowly and with a calm voice. Use silences to to emphasise specific parts.

At the end, recap shortly with a louder, clear voice and add more excitement to your voice as you put them to work.

Your voice is one of your most important tools. Think about the impact of the voice of people like Morgan Freeman, Anthony Hopkins or David Attenborough when they narrate a documentary. Pay attention to how they play with their voice to keep you intrigued and engaged. You can use the same techniques. When you are facilitating online sessions, it makes all the difference.

Experiment 3 / ORCHESTRATE

During conversation when some valuable points are being made by the participants ...

- Pay close attention: hunt for contradictions, different interpretations, important nuances, controversies.
- Intervene with determination: do not hesitate. Disrupt the flow to direct the attention towards the point someone made and add a trigger question.
- Trigger with an open question: make sure you do not make any suggestions or influence opinions. Ask open questions like 'How does this statement compare with our earlier conclusion?'
- Continue the conversation: call someone by their first name and ask them to respond, preferably the person with a strong opinion to fuel the conversation.
- Observe the effect: observe the response and ask some more participants to build on it. Then let the conversation take its course again.

Beware: the timing of the intervention, or the topic, can disrupt the flow of conversation too much and cause confusion. To avoid this, you need to be to the point and avoid drawing too much attention to yourself. As soon as you have intervened, direct the attention towards each other by calling out different people to contribute with their thoughts. Otherwise, you become part of the conversation, and that is not the intention of orchestration. You are not supposed to play an instrument.

Experiment 4 / LEVERAGE DIVERSITY

When a diverse group of participants are sharing their thoughts ...

Try to remember everyone's background and expertise and intentionally ask the opinion of specific participants referring to their background, experience or skillset. Especially when they can provide a completely new perspective, a different way of looking at the topic, a twist to the conversation that may lead to a breakthrough.

Often, it is not enough just to invite a diverse group of participants to have qualitative multi-perspective conversations. You need to prompt people to bring their specific expertise or knowledge to the table. Pay attention to the difference between the participants and amplify those different perspectives at the right time during the session.

Experiment 5 / TRY OUT SOME NEW GROUND RULES

Before your next session …

- evaluate the interaction and collaboration of your previous session(s);
- indicate what could have been better;
- identify what was missing or working against you;
- come up with a new ground rule to improve the collaboration or interaction.

A ground rule could be promoting certain behaviour, it could be referencing a ritual (for example a reflection ritual), it could be a practical agreement (for example coming back on time after a break). Whatever you would like to try out, suggest it in a positive and open way. It should not feel like a restrictive rule, rather a supportive guideline.

8. Catalyse

How do you get commitment from your participants?

Catalyse is the inspirational side of facilitation. From this chapter, you will learn that ownership is the result of good facilitation. I often notice that people struggle with ensuring execution and implementation of all the output from their meetings and workshops. Especially when applying methods like Design Thinking, it seems to be hard to execute new ideas. What execution needs is ownership. Facilitators are needed to catalyse teams for this ownership – or commitment.

Catalysing is about creating a sense of ownership amongst your participants. This sense of ownership goes along with a sense of belonging and significance. Being at the right place, at the right time, when your skills, your experience, your personality, your whole person fits the challenge or purpose. That is when you feel you can contribute. That is when you feel you can make a difference, that you can have impact.

We are all faced with fundamental questions like: 'Why am I here?' and 'What should I be doing here then?' We have similar questions when joining into a shared moment of co-creation. In everything we do, we have the urge to figure out what the point is: 'Should I actually be part of this?' As a facilitator and architect of the shared moment, it is your privilege to answer those existential questions – within the context of your session. When your participants feel that they are onto something, when they feel they can make a difference and that they are an important part of the team, they will get a sense of ownership. This also applies on an organizational level, and even on a society level. But in a shared moment, this feeling can be evoked by the facilitator.

Why am I here? Shaping the purpose of the gathering is probably the most important starting point when setting up a session. It is your role as the facilitator to find the relevance for the type of participants and the context. You might say it is about finding the 'hook' to get the participants emotionally invested in the gathering. The hook needs to be crisp and clear. It immediately communicates why it is worth it to put time and effort into the session, but more importantly, it also intentionally excludes many things that are *not* the focus of the session.

If the hook is confusing and covers a too broad or undefined area, you cannot expect participants to feel that they can make a difference. If it is too narrow or banal, participants may feel that there is no impact to be made.

In order for participants to become emotionally invested, the purpose also needs to be genuine. They need to care about the outcome. It is a form of relevance that provides meaning to their efforts. Usually, participants do not get very excited if the desired outcome is more profit for the shareholders. It is often forgotten that the participants are key stakeholders as well. Making their stake explicit within the goals of the workshop works better.

The purpose needs to be genuine.

When I start a session, right before lift-off, I usually have an honest conversation with the group about what the purpose really means to them. I ask each of the participants to share how they interpret the purpose of the session, and what part of it really speaks to them. Think of it as an 'ownership check-in'.

When there is a human-centered purpose, people can easily become invested. As a facilitator, it makes sense to investigate what the human impact of potential outcomes might be. Then you tie that back into the purpose. Let me give you an example. I work closely with the Design Thinkers Academy in Amsterdam. One of their most popular courses is the week-long bootcamp where a group of people learn how to solve a challenge from a human-centered perspective. These challenges are often real challenges, coming from the academy's partners.

FIND A HUMAN-CENTERED HOOK

One of the more recent challenges was about 'How to deal with organizational matters in healthcare during a crisis?' After doing some research, the challenge was adapted to focus on patients with a chronic illness, and how they depended on was scaled down because of the COVID crisis. The solution that came out of the process: a collaboration with retired physicians serving as back-up to deal with the demand. The enthusiasm of the partner, who brought this challenge into the bootcamp, encouraged the course participants to work further on detailing it out, even after the course ended. A regional paper even wrote an article about the idea. These solutions came from a Design Thinking course, where people just gathered because serendipity brought them there. There were no extrinsic rewards or prizes to be won. Ownership was purely driven by the participants' emotional investment. This is how a human-centered hook for your purpose can help to drive commitment amongst the participants.

What should I be doing here then? That is another good question. People are not always aware of the value they bring to a gathering. Most of us are modest about our knowledge and skills. It is a big world out there, so it is easy to feel intimidated and insignificant. But having observed people from the sideline, as a facilitator, I can tell you we are capable of mind-blowing achievements together. I have enjoyed moments when people generated new ideas together that were just plain genius. I have seen people feeling such deep empathy it was almost heartbreaking. I have seen people inspiring each other in conversation as if they were singing a song in harmony. I have seen participants feeling deep appreciation for each other just for sharing an amazing moment of exchanging thoughts.

A facilitator can acknowledge contributions from participants and link their efforts back to the overall purpose. By making sure each participant is aware of their value to the group, they will start to feel significant. And when people understand they can be a meaningful part of a group of people building something meaningful together, they will start to feel commitment to the team and the purpose. First, they need to believe in the cause, then they need to believe in themselves. The result is ownership of their role in the project. As a facilitator, you are instrumental in achieving this.

HOW TO MEASURE COMMITMENT

Over the years, I have developed a very simple way to measure commitment at the end of a meeting or a workshop. It helps me to understand whether I managed to be a good catalyst during the session. It works as follows: I present an empty poster, or an empty frame in the virtual world, for all participants to fill in at the end of the session. First, I ask them to write down at least three actions they could take, in their capacity, to help build on the output of the session. This could be about checking feasibility of a decided approach, contacting a potential partner, getting buy-in from a key stakeholder or testing some ideas with a customer. When everyone has added their action points and explained them to the group, I ask all participants to indicate which action point from another participant they would like to help with and connect on after the session. When all participants have indicated where they want to help, I start a sharing round so everyone can explain how they would like to support the other participant's action points. And especially: *why*.

This type of wrap-up provides actionable closure for everyone involved. It closes the loop of all the work done during the session. You start a session using specific input. Then you drive participation and engagement from all participants to leverage the diversity of perspectives and talents to end up at a desired output. The actionable closure creates commitment to build on the output by linking capabilities to action points and openly supporting these actions.

Actionable closure is a great way to reveal the actual level of commitment in the end. I have facilitated sessions where participants could not stop writing down action points. The provided white space was too small to hold all their great intentions. I had to ask them to add their initials or use a certain color to keep track of who was writing what. In such a case, everyone is completely committed to the purpose. From the level of participation and engagement during the session, I can usually tell what the potential level of commitment is. And by engaging in quality conversation, participants usually already get hints about their possible action points after the session. As a facilitator I can nurture that commitment even more by acknowledging the great things they are bringing to the table and by congratulating them when the group gets to a breakthrough.

Skepticism is the absolute enemy of catalysing.

Pointing out the value of an insight, a thought or a great interpretation makes people aware of it. Making them aware of the value of their contribution works as a catalyst, making them want to provide even more valuable contributions. Eventually they will grow an eagerness to see the project through even after the session. They are starting to own it, fueled by energy to take action. Right after the session, I already see emails flying back and forth about the action points.

It can be challenging to catalyse for commitment. I have facilitated workshops where participants lacked trust towards each other, towards the organization and management. As a facilitator, I can try to fix the trust towards each other. I can even get them to engage fully. But if they do not buy into the purpose, I will have a really hard time catalysing for commitment. For example, when I would acknowledge a great contribution, the participant would appreciate it, but then they say: 'Well that's great, I know, but really, I already know it will not change the situation. We have tried and failed so many times before.'

Even if I would emphasize the purpose and meaning of each step in the session, I could almost hear them thinking 'Yeah right, I wish!' with every new idea.

EVERYTHING STARTS WITH THE PURPOSE

These experiences have made it very clear to me that participation and engagement can create a false image of commitment to a facilitator. At the end of the session, I would bring up the empty frame and ask everyone to fill in at least three action points. As time ticked by, I only noticed a few points being added. Not even one per participant. Out of courtesy, some would put their name in to support some of the few action points. Some participants who did not add one single action point, would not even add their name to anything. When I called them out to check whether they would like to reconsider, they would often say 'Oh no, I'm just here to experience the session and learn, it is not in my 'role' (they meant intention) to actually follow up with action points.' This does not provide a proper feeling of closure. It will not help to get commitment and ownership, and it is a very clear sign that there is more going on that needs fixing.

Sometimes it is just not enough to shape the relevance of the purpose to make it strong and exciting. Sometimes you also need some bigwigs to come in and reinforce the importance of the purpose. But if people do not buy it, if they think that their efforts will not make a difference – no matter what the group is capable of – you need to figure out what is causing their skepticism. If there is an underlying issue causing skepticism, you need to try to solve

Everything starts with the purpose. And the purpose always has context.

this beforehand. Or at least prepare yourself to be faced with skepticism, the absolute enemy of catalysing. Just remember, everything starts with the purpose. And the purpose always has context.

CATALYSING TO GET COMMITMENT

There are three practices that have helped me to be a catalyst in order to increase commitment. These three aspects will help you to keep all participants emotionally invested in the cause of the gathering. And it will help them to find out how they can best contribute during the session. As with Guiding (Chapter 6) and Conducting (Chapter 7), keep your captain's log at hand while reading. And keep it at hand while trying them out during your facilitation efforts. I will explain them from my own experience, so just use them as inspiration and make them your own.

1. **A purpose to start with.** The purpose makes all the effort worthwhile. A facilitator needs to fuel the momentum of the session frequently, by reminding everyone of the purpose, oiling the spinning wheels.

2. **Coach, not couch.** When everyone is participating intensely in the session, the facilitator cannot be a 'couch potato' watching from the sideline. A facilitator can catalyse by coaching and acknowledging valuable contributions.

3. **Make it fit.** Even with a good purpose and great coaching, people can still feel out of place. They need to feel they matter in order to feel ownership.

1. A purpose to start with

Every element of your narrative, every step in your plan, should feed into the overall purpose of the session. Every part has its own value to help the team move towards the desired output. It can be very enthusing and encouraging for all participants to be reminded each time of how the next step in the journey will help the group to make progress.

I call this practice 'big purpose – small purpose'. At the start of any stepping-stone, the facilitator reminds all participants again what the overall reason is to spend time together (big purpose), and why it makes sense to take the upcoming step (small purpose). Every step of the way you add meaning. And step by step you build their commitment to take responsibility for the overall purpose.

It does not only work well at the start of each step. It is also a great antidote against criticism. In the previous chapter, I described to you two ways to minimize the influence of disturbing or very critical participants: grouping into smaller teams and breaking comments open for the group to respond to. 'Big purpose – small purpose' is an extra round of ammunition to deal with participants who keep questioning the narrative.

So how do you apply 'big purpose – small purpose' to get even the most critical participants aligned? When a participant expresses concerns about the program or next step, first, I 'Bruce Lee' them. I you would like to refresh your memory ont his impressive move I borrowed from martial arts, revisit page 80 of Chapter 1. After the Bruce Lee, I serve a well-placed 'big purpose – small purpose'. I give a reminder of why we are spending our time together, and then tie in the reason why we should jointly engage in the next step. It leads to the question whether they are convinced of the value of this next step. If they question the value, I will first ask them to explain why, trying to empathize with the participant. Then I break it open to the group to consider the importance of the argumentation. If the collective mind does not agree with the comments, then I invite them to explain how the next step could help (do not explain it yourself).

If the group agrees with the comments, things become a bit slippery. It is necessary to have a quick reflection with the group about what might be missing from the narrative. Then I adapt the narrative on the spot or install a break or a solo working moment for the participants, so I can take a few minutes to improvise how to best move forward. When ready to move forward with the changed plans, I bring in 'big purpose – small purpose' again to connect the revised next step with the overall purpose and generate enthusiasm for lift-off.

You might feel the need to adapt the program, even if no one is expressing concerns. For example, when you suddenly realize the next activity might be too overwhelming for the group and you do not want to

The glue that holds your narrative together is the meaning you add to each step.

lose momentum. When you adapt your program openly, you need to reconnect everyone back to the session, using 'big purpose – small purpose'. It shows that your role is to help the collective make progress on the shared purpose in the best way. It shows you are there to serve them, not to impose your program. Showing vulnerability and honesty about changing the program, reinstates your trust-worthiness as a facilitator. Check whether every-one feels okay to move forward with the changed plans and get the team back on track.

Being the guardian of space is the same thing as being the guardian of purpose. The space you have created for the participants – the shared moment – only exists because of the purpose. If the purpose is weak, the moment is fragile. If the purpose is strong, the moment can be intense. In other words, the quality of the moment you create for all invitees, depends on the quality of the purpose. The glue that holds your narrative together is the meaning you add to each step, tied into the overall purpose.

By repeating the 'big purpose – small purpose' you keep intensifying that shared moment and increase commitment.

2. Coach, not couch

The way I coach as a facilitator is called 'MOH'. It reminds me I have to do it 'more'. MOH stands for <u>m</u>irror, <u>o</u>pen and <u>h</u>onour.

Mirror. By mirroring, I help the team or a participant to look back at a contribution and see the value it added to the conversation and the ses-sion. I do not just repeat it. I really mirror it, meaning I explain exactly what happened:

'Cindy brought up the idea of removing this extra checkpoint to admit a visitor to the museum. Then we had Tony and Ellen explain how we could check the admittance requirements at another checkpoint using this new technology they are testing. And now John suggested this new entry flow that will probably cut the waiting times in half. This means that you might have found a way to increase customer satisfaction significantly, considering that David earlier shared how visitors struggle most with the long queues. Your different viewpoints and ideas brought us to some valuable conclusions. We can build on this in our next step'.

Mirroring is about painting a picture of what just happened. Often, participants are not aware of the great exchange of thoughts and knowledge that led to another way of looking at things. They may take it for granted or underestimate the power of the quality conversation they just had. Mirroring makes them aware of the synergy in the space.

Open. When I 'open it up', I look for other participants credit someone's contribution or an achievement of the group. It is not always most impactful if the facilitator acknowledges an achievement. I am the first to admit I can really overdo it. My acknowledgements can come across as exaggerated. Often, it feels more authentic when you have someone from the team show appreciation. 'Maria, can you tell us, how did we get to this breakthrough moment? And where did the key insight come from?' You could trigger some more acknowledgement by asking afterwards if everyone feels the same. Or you could ask if anyone wants to add any recognition for the team or a person in particular. Opening it up can increase that sense of belonging in a group. It makes people feel acknowledged for a contribution by their team members. Again, it increases commitment to the purpose and the team.

When I choose that perfect moment to open it up, I first observe whether participants are getting excited about any input from others, or whether they are surprised by a sudden turning point or tipping point. I use that moment's energy to open it up for acknowledgement and give the team a boost. Keep it short and simple. Spending too much time on acknowledging can break the flow of the session.

Keep it short and simple.

Honour. The 'H' in 'MOH' stands for honouring a single contribution from a participant or an achievement of the team. If you have been guiding well, you should have gained a good amount of trust from the team. You can use your established position as a facilitator when honoring something someone said. It is just as simple as 'may I point out for a minute that this was a very valid point from Steph, thanks for that, and because of this important insight you were all able to conclude …' It sounds like your directing attention towards the point Steph is making, just like with orchestration. The only difference here is that you are honoring the point after the group has already shared and processed it. That way, you can make sure the point has really made an impact before you honor it.

In summary, *mirroring* is a way of acknowledging a team's performance by replaying what just happened. *Opening* is a way of having the team members acknowledge each other's contributions. And *honouring* is a way for the facilitator to call out a great contribution. Mirroring and opening are perfect practices to apply at a moment of closure. Honoring can be applied multiple times during the session. MOH(re) MOH-ing is always a great idea to catalyze the group into commitment.

3. Make it fit

Skepticism, overwhelm and boredom. These are the three villains that make it hard for a facilitator to be a catalyst for the group. While skepticism is related to purpose and meaning, overwhelm and boredom are related to the program. Overwhelm and boredom decrease commitment. On the other hand, when you specifically connect skills and talents to certain activities of a program, it will generate commitment.

The following example will show you how adapting the program and connecting individual capabilities can catalyze for commitment.

A while ago, I facilitated a workshop where the participants were asked to empathize with hospital patients. The goal was improving a specific hospital experience. My aim was to add more depth into their conversations by stirring up their empathy for the patients. I repeatedly reminded them of the patient persona they collectively described at the start of the workshop. But somehow, they just could not understand the patient's reality beyond their own perspective. The conversations just went on and on about the fact that the patients did not like to wait, in uncertainty, for their test results.

But there were more insights in the described persona, providing a more in-depth understanding of the key needs of the patients, beyond waiting in uncertainty. When we got to the point where they needed to decide which was the most significant challenge for the patient, I asked them again to review their persona description before sharing their thoughts, one by one. But I noticed fatigue and boredom. They felt that they had done this multiple times before. It made me realize I was stretching their patience and that I urgently needed to change my strategy.

I immediately called for a ten minute break. We knew from investigating the patient's journey, there were some difficult interaction moments between the medical staff and the patients. I also noticed some extroverted participants who had a vivid imagination and a lot of patient-facing experience, having spent time working at hospitals. During the ten minutes, I created smaller teams, making sure each team had one of the 'patient-facing' participants, and prepared for a different next step. After the break, I announced to break out into those smaller teams. I explained how each team had at least one participant with patient-facing experience. This person could provide a reality check every time the team imagined the type of emotions and behavior of the patients. I also asked for one participant to take up the role of the 'persona-representative'. This person had to remind everyone of the persona description, to help direct the line of thinking of the team. Finally, I briefed each team to choose the most difficult interaction moment in the patient journey and prepare a role play of that moment to share with the group.

After some preparation time, we had three smaller teams roleplaying what they thought was the hardest part in the patient's experience. It became a turning point. Suddenly, all kinds of stories and personal references were unlocked. The teams had perfectly depicted what the reality of the patient looked like, along with all accompanying emotions and even quotes. I changed the schedule to allow for a more time to share and discuss the roleplaying. We did not end up with solutions at the end of that session, which was the output initially expected. But we did end up with a much better understanding of what we really needed to solve for those patients. It was not necessarily about waiting in uncertainty. It turned out that patients expected to wait in uncertainty and were prepared to do so – even though it was not pleasant. The real issue was the nature of the interaction when they received the results, and the complexity of the information they received. The change in the program did not only bring new energy, but several participants also came up with potential action points for after the session.

Improvising and adapting your narrative during a session to avoid over-whelm or boredom can have a serious impact on gaining commitment. The tricky part is noticing it soon enough to do something about it. It is such a shame to spend all that effort in the moment, only to realize at the end that there had been no real commitment from the start.

With every break you give, you create a window for yourself.

If you notice it in time, you can still adapt the program to best fit the skill set and comfort lev-el. When I arrive at a situation where I need to adapt on the spot, I create a 'window of time' for myself as a facilitator. With every break you give, or when you ask people to gather their thoughts individually for a couple of minutes, you create a window for yourself to reflect on the journey so far and prepare – or even change – the next steps. By creating this window, you will maintain a good level of trust and comfort to ensure a smooth con-tinuation of activities and conversations.

As explained in the example, there are two aspects to catalyzing: on one hand, it is about avoiding overwhelm and boredom by adapting your pro-gram. On the other hand, it includes identifying specific skills, strengths or knowledge that certain participants have and leveraging these capab-ilities by connecting them to program. By noticing people's capabil-ities and helping them apply them to benefit the team, you are again acknowledging their value for the team and the purpose. Making it fit helps to drive ownership and commitment.

PREPARE FOR SUCCESS

How do you prepare for successful catalyzing, as a facilitator? You need to prepare for full commitment by making sure you have a compelling and straightforward purpose for the gathering. You also need to assess all the potential risks and pitfalls of your session. And last, but certainly not least, you need to align with all the key stakeholders about what success looks like.

Prepare for purpose

'Guide, Conduct and Catalyse' can be applied to any type of meeting, workshop or session. You can even apply elements of the 'holy trinity' during a one-on-one with a colleague or a direct report. In any case, the success always starts with the purpose. This is a fact, simply because you cannot create ownership without a compelling purpose. And ownership is what you need to create outcomes from the output of your session.

The purpose is like an elevator pitch. You cannot cover everything. It needs to be focused, and you need to be able to explain it in just a few sentences. If the purpose is fuzzy, the meeting will start fuzzily. For the record, fuzzy is not necessarily the same thing as difficult or paradoxical. By fuzzy I mean that the purpose is unclear, explained in a long-winded way or cluttered with irrelevant topics. Often, this happens to make it sound important, or to make it sound relevant to an army of stakeholders. Fuzziness does not lead to ownership. Your purpose is the starting point of *everything*.

Outlook – or any other email software – should add an extra box in the header of an invitation email. Underneath 'subject', 'location' and 'duration' it should say (in capitals): 'PURPOSE OF THE MEETING'. And the box right next to it should only allow for a maximum amount of characters, to make sure it stays crisp and clear.

The purpose of a gathering can be described in several ways. One of the most popular approaches is to state it as a challenge, starting with 'How might we …', this is called the HMW statement. For example: 'How might we help patients with a chronic illness to receive sufficient care during a healthcare crisis when available medical staff is limited'. It can be very effective to state it as a challenge because this will give it the undertone of co-creating a better outcome together.

The purpose can also be established without using any specific structure, but it is always contextual. There is a history, a current situation and a desired future state. So, when you are thinking about the purpose of your next catch-up meeting with your team, think about everything that happened up until now, what the current status is, and what you would like to work towards after the catch-up.

Even a simple catch-up can have a more compelling purpose than merely catching up. It may be about synchronizing the to-do's and agendas so you have a shared timeline to reach milestones. Or it could be about aligning what to do with all stakeholders, reviewing the current status of the project and listing up which stakeholder should be part of which future step. It could be anything more focused than just catching up. When you write down your purpose, consider the following characteristics:

→ Focus, do not leave it up to chance, try not to talk about everything, prioritise beforehand (what is it not about?).

→ Use plain language, avoid any jargon that might not be understood by everyone.

→ Give straightforward reasons why it is worth the time: what is the type of output to achieve a clear outcome?

→ Provide a filtered-out context, with immediate relevance, not a long historical explanation.

→ Leave enough room for different opinions and expressions, the output should not be defined in detail upfront. Otherwise, it is 'rigged' from the start.

→ Have empathy for the invitees. How is it relevant to their work?

→ Make it compelling for them.

Whenever I ponder the right purpose for a session, I always start thinking about the road that got us there, and how everyone experienced that road. And I try to get a really clear view on where we are at the moment, and what everyone's opinion about this current status is. I think about facts and imagine related emotions. I also think about who is currently working on what, and what has been decided or shared lately. Then, I envision what the road ahead might look like, and how it fits into the bigger scheme of things. This bigger scheme consist of long-term goals or trends or evolutions or aspirations. This thought process always helps me to finally nail down the strongest wording to get all invitees on board and ready to get emotionally invested in the cause.

Define success

When the purpose is clear, the next big question is 'How can we spend that time with each other successfully?' Or in other words, 'What does success look like to the involved crew and key stakeholders?' This is an all-encompassing question I try to get answered beforehand when talking those to involved. It reveals the underlying motivation that underpins the purpose and the output. The purpose inspires with context and focus. It speaks to our imagination. The output makes it very practical and tangible. It gives us a concrete reason to spend time together. The definition of success gives us aspiration. It provides possibilities by showing us a picture of what outcome might come from the planned output.

When asking the question of what success looks like to the owner of a project or the organizer of the meeting, I often get answers like:

> *'It's a success if all these involved stakeholders buy into the same plan of approach at the end of the session.'*

> *'It's a success if these people actually decide to do something about it.'*

> *'We're happy if we end up with a much more in-depth, shared, understanding of the real struggle these unfortunate people are experiencing, so we know where to focus our efforts first.'*

> *'We're there if we made it so tangible that we can go out and test it after this session.'*

> *'It is a success if we are able to resolve our issues and recognize ourselves again as a strong team.'*

> *'It was worth it if it keeps fueling this great momentum we're having, and everyone remains excited to do the work.'*

> *'It's a success if I see a glimpse of meaning again in my job.'*

> *'If we all understand why we're going to make a difference with this new product.'*

> *'If our partners get on board and want to provide us with necessary resources.'*

What do these examples have in common? Some goal of coherence between the involved participants, putting a clear stake in the ground again, kickstarting some important actions together. And these actions lead to aspirational outcomes that feed into some impactful vision. Maybe the vision is not always mentioned, and the outcome can still be a bit unclear, but 'coming together to take action' is always there to define success.

Even though the essence of what success means is pretty similar each time, the nuances are. And those nuances are not incredibly important to pick up on as a facilitator. They will reveal the underlying challenges. When you get answers to your success question, the hesitation, the wording, the tone of voice or the points that are emphasized, can tell you that the team might not be collaborating very well. Or management might not be in full support, another department or team might be competing for the same resources, they have absolutely no clue how to approach their challenge, etc.

So, when you ask what success means, you explore the possibility of success as a facilitator. An open focus and deep listening might reveal knowledge about sensitivities that can make or break your session.

Assess risks and pitfalls

When you know the purpose and the definition of success, you have a good sense of the potential commitment from all participants to build on the output and achieve a desired outcome. But there are pirates and sea monsters in the waters. Polish your cannon balls and sharpen your blades, captaineering is not for the faint-hearted.

There are many variables that can feast on commitment, nibbling on it until there is none left. The same basic mechanism applies: to maintain open focus you need to your participants manage themselves and manage their stress triggers. A narrow focus can cause a drop in coherence. And less openness will lead to less understanding.

Managing the variables that cause narrow focus is easier said than done. Let me show you the general variables I am always mindful of when preparing for success. It will help you to watch out for sea monsters.

Biased facilitation. When you are emotionally invested in the output of the session, you run the risk of wearing multiple hats during your session. The way you direct the attention might be influenced by your own opinion without you even being aware of it. This can lead to mistrust and disengagement.

Conflicting or unrealistic expectations. The goals and purpose of a session should be agreed upon beforehand amongst the key stakeholders and all participants. If participants are not convinced that their participation is required or that useful output will be achieved, it will have a negative effect on their engagement in the session.

Too little time, goals too big. Quality conversations take time. If the desired output cannot be achieved properly in the allocated time, agree on a different time frame upfront. The level of participation depends on the time experience you create. And the level of engagement depends on the smooth orchestration within that timeframe.

When you ask what success means, you explore the possibility of success as a facilitator.

Participants only having time for part of the session. When attendees only join for part of the session, you need to make sure their attendance is beneficial for the session. It is best for them to be present at a lift-off and stay until the closure of a part, to avoid disruption by leaving mid-activity or mid-conversation.

Partial remote participation. When part of the group sits in the same room and some people dial in from a remote location, it is hard to have smooth quality conversations. People sitting face-to-face will naturally address their attention more to each other than to the other 'online' participants. In my experience it works best to bring everything online or everything offline. Another solution is to split the group in an online team and an offline team and have them work separately with frequent group sharing moments.

Participants cannot express themselves comfortably in the chosen language. If the chosen language is not everyone's native tongue, you need to check how comfortable everyone is with expressing themselves in that language. You might even want to invite everyone to give the non-native speakers more space and time to express themselves and support them to get their point across.

Sponsor/leadership wants to join. Involving very senior people in sessions can have a serious effect on the openness between participants. It can feel threatening, even if this leader has a very open communication style. As a facilitator, you have a wildcard. You should be able to have a very open and honest conversation with the person in the leadership position. Is their perspective, knowledge and expertise necessary to get to great output? Will their presence threaten the safe space? If they are not sure, do we want to take that risk? What is the leader's intention for participating? Any form of control should be avoided in any facilitated session. It would just mean a lot more work for the facilitator to continuously neutralize that control and regain openness.

Difficulty blending personalities. When you do the diversity check, you can come to the conclusion that there are conflicting personalities and needs in the room. Prepare yourself for some intense guiding, conducting and catalyzing. Obviously, you can make it easier on yourself by questioning the composition of the invited team while trying to keep the necessary diversity. But often you do not have the necessary information upfront. Consider those moments of intense facilitation as great learning opportunities to grow. But make sure you can keep your own state managed. In part 3, I will give you all kinds of tips on how to manage your own state during challenging facilitation.

Similar work done by other teams. When digging for the purpose, make sure you pay enough attention to all the workstreams that have been done, or are ongoing. If there are conflicting workstreams, try to get the organizers to align with the other team first. Maybe even encourage them to bring in the expertise from the other team. It will force the organizers to find a purpose for this meeting that is complimentary to the work already done by others. It unites everyone, which is a much more productive way to get to good output. If the competition remains, it will possibly lead to a narrow focus when there is confrontation at some point. It can also decrease the belief of the involved team that their output will make any difference. They will be less committed and reluctant to execute afterwards.

Participants without experience with tools and methods. How do you facilitate when the participants have no knowledge of the applied methodology? I get this question often when giving courses. First of all, tools and methods should never be a goal in itself. Any tool or method you apply in your narrative needs to be adapted to the team, time and place. If the steps in your narrative are meaningful and actionable, then you are building ownership. If you blindly install tools in your session, without considering whether they are daunting or meaningless to your participants, you can forget about their commitment. If you are not sure about the match between existing tools and the knowledge of the team, simplify the tools to only some key questions. In the end, any tool is built on some questions to guide a thought process. Think about how you can trigger the right thought processes in a more simple and straightforward way.

I often simplify customer journey tools. Such tools often consist of the different steps in the journey in vertical columns, and the emotional state, goals, context, touchpoints, needs and obstacle, in horizontal lanes across the vertical columns. At first glance this may look complex and intimidating. As an alternative, in offline workshops, I ask the participants to write up the different steps horizontally, and add some insights on emotions, context and goals in each column, without using a tool. Starting out with white space and visualizing the thought process step by step often feels more encouraging. At the end, often the team is amazed by their visual accomplishment.

These are pitfalls I often come across when being asked to facilitate. I am sure there are a lot more to be mindful of. Your captain's log is where you can keep track of them. Open the log every time you are asked to facilitate. Go over the risks you have experienced before and evaluate whether they are relevant in the given case.

A CATALYST FOR OWNERSHIP

Now you know that you can only prepare for success when you understand what success means to the people involved. Purpose and a vision of success will help you to get commitment. But there are always obstacles that can nibble away on the commitment. As a catalyst, you can prepare for the sea monsters: use purpose to encourage the participants, MOH (mirroring, opening, honouring) them into 'fame'. This is how you make sure the participants will own the output and take it forward towards a desired outcome.

Captain's Log

Are you ready to build on your catalyzing skills? Experiment with these five practices and keep track of all your learnings in your captain's log. Pay close attention to any increase in commitment amongst your participants.

Experiment 1 / BIG PURPOSE - SMALL PURPOSE

At the beginning of your session – and at the start of any new 'stage' in your session – when you feel you need to recalibrate the focus of the participants …

1. explain context: any information on the current situation and what brought us here together, any information about previous work done on this topic or how the previous stage feeds into the next;
2. refer to the overall purpose: what are we solving or what is the kind of output we are working towards and why (big purpose);
3. make the immediate next step meaningful, describe how the following step will help to reach our goals (small purpose);
4. give instructions for the immediate next step.

When you often give meaning to the gathering and the task at hand, your participants will feel more motivated to participate, engage and even committed to take action after the session.

Experiment 2 / MOH

At the end of an important discussion, at a breakthrough moment during your session, when a participant shares an interesting insight or draws an eye-opening conclusion …

Mirror: describe an exact replay of the conversation that led to the breakthrough moment, using the first names of everyone who contributed.

For example: *'Let me quickly summarise what just happened, Mark started by saying … then Jess added … to which Margaret replied that from her experience ... and as a result everyone agreed that .... And this conclusion now brings us to the point ...'*

Make sure to add in some appropriate adjectives (*insightful, sharp, original, unconventional, fresh, clarifying, rich, enlightening, valid, well founded, thoughtful*) and even a few superlatives (*excellent, exceptional, extraordinary, most surprising, most unexpected, cleverest*) to emphasize the value of each contribution.

Open it up: prompt a participant to acknowledge and appreciate the contribution of another participant.

For example: *'Hey John, can you share which opinion, and from whom, you identify most with?' or 'Tell me, what do you like most about the idea that Sophie just shared?'*

By prompting the participants to express appreciation towards each other you build trust within the team. This trust will open everyone up even more and participants might even start sharing their appreciation towards each other's idea without you having to prompt it.

Honour: express your appreciation as a facilitator.

For example: *'That insight made a real difference in helping us to come up with this new interpretation, thank you for sharing Lena!' or 'That was an intense but fruitful conversation, with good collaborative effort, well done, you have earned a break.'*

Authenticity is essential. If you throw around too many compliments, no one will believe you anymore. Make sure there is an obvious reason to express appreciation. It could even be more effective if you mention the reason clearly: 'That is a completely different perspective which might explain why our target audience behaves in such a way. Thank you so much for explaining, Monica. Who would like to build on this new insight?'

Experiment 3 / CREATE A HOOK

During your preparation, make the purpose of the session sound meaningful and worth the effort. Here are some tips to create a persuasive 'hook' when sharing the purpose with your invitees …

1. **Use a provocative question:** it is relevant, it triggers people's curiosity and it does not have an easy answer, like: 'What is the biggest blind spot we have about our customer?'
2. **Use a quote:** it needs to be real, controversial, and coming from a reliable and respected source ('After my onboarding I honestly had no clue where to start and no one to ask.' Senior Vice President HR)
3. **Use a fact or stat:** it does not need a lot of interpretation, just make sure it is surprising and clearly linked to the topic of your session ('did you know that 80% of our customers would switch to a competitive brand if they were only 5% cheaper?').
4. **Use leadership endorsement:** it adds weight to the topic, clearly links to a strategic goal, it provides context ('To reach our two-year goal of connecting all our products to one single platform, we need to understand how … which is why this series of workshops can really help us to …').
5. **Use empathy:** it is personal, it hits a sensitive spot, it unites ('We have all been struggling with spending hours in back-to-back online meetings for months, using the worst video platforms and outdated virtual workspaces, going to sleep with headaches and sore eyes …').
6. **Use visual proof (when available):** it is self-explanatory, it is high quality/high resolution, it speaks a thousand words (for example, add a face to a testimonial, show a picture of the consequences of a problem or show a picture which gives an idea of the potential consequences of a problem)

It is always a good idea to include the hook in your invitation to the session, and it has even more impact of you repeat or expand on the hook at the beginning of your session, especially if you can make it visual.

Experiment 4 / UNDERSTAND SUCCESS

When there are multiple key stakeholders and they have their own nuanced vision of success …

- Make a list of the key stakeholders and identify their 'stake'
- Plan a short call with each key stakeholder
- Ask about their perspective on context, important issues, potential improvements and expectations
- Explain how you will take their input into account (do not make any promises about the output)

Plan short moments with the key stakeholders to make sure that the conversation is limited to only relevant information about 'stake' and expectations. Then decide whether you need to plan more time with any of them for a more in-depth conversation. You only need to understand the essence of what they are looking for and remain an observer and enabler rather than expressing your opinion and possibly making any promises about the output. If you create expectations about the specific output and generate an opinion about the topic, that could lead to biased facilitation. if you are not ate biased in the way you facilitate, you may lose trust from the team which will prevent you from properly conducting the dialogue or driving ownership.

Experiment 5 / ASSESS RISKS

Every time you facilitate any type of gathering, assess risks and pitfalls by investigating these things (upfront) …

- experience of each participant with your type of session: online or offline collaboration, topic of the session;
- other workstreams on this topic: leverage them or clearly differentiate your session;
- expectations from different key stakeholders: identify conflicts and try to resolve them upfront;
- timing with all participants: avoid the disruption of people coming in late, skipping parts or leaving early;
- titles and positions: make sure no one feels intimidated or holds back because of leadership participants;
- agreements with leadership: have them blend in perfectly with the rest of the team in case they participate;
- your stake: are you in any way emotionally invested in the outcome, can you facilitate without influencing, otherwise become a participant and assign someone to facilitate;

- expected outcome: get clear on what kind of work still needs to be done after the session and who will be assigned to make it happen.

Preparation is everything. If you want to feel confident about your facilitation, take your time to investigate all the ins and outs first. It will be much easier to foresee potential difficulties if you understand the context and the people involved.

Closure

Facilitation is the purest form of leadership

In facilitation, there are no egos involved, there is no status to be maintained, no 'leader'-image to live up to. It is purely about getting the best out of people. A facilitator is 'giving' by holding space for others to become a coherent group of people. A facilitator has no hidden agenda, and does not require specific output from the team.

A FACILITATOR DOES NOT take ownership of the output or the potential outcome. It is not their role. Their sole responsibility is to be the guardian of the space and the owner of time, and to let the team thrive in their shared moment.

Taking on this responsibility, a facilitator can guide for participation, conduct for engagement and catalyze for commitment. Participation comes from trust; engagement comes from directing attention and managing energy; and commitment results in ownership. In other words, you are building a safe space for people to openly build on each other so they can find their way forward with strong intention.

In Part 1, I explained to you how this productive safe space rarely results organically in co-creation. Guide, Conduct and Catalyze can bring about real change and unite people around some great causes. It is a springboard, an inspiring framework that will hopefully give you the confidence to step up and be a captain.

Facilitation is a lifelong learning journey. You can create your own style, your own approach. I am not sure if you will ever be able to call it mastery, but you can be sure that you will have made a dent in the universe by trying to become a master at it. It is a brave thing to try and be a selfless leader who just wants to help people to get the best out of a shared moment. Just for trying, you deserve that respectful title of captain.

In the next part, I will summarize all the aspects to prepare for successful guiding, conducting and catalyzing, in a four-step model. This model provides a simple, structured approach to get ready for any type of session. An easy and effective way to prepare yourself helps build your confidence to facilitate.

The last chapter of Part 3 will explain how you can own your session by managing your state. This is the final step in building your facilitative confidence. It provides tools to manage your emotions, your energy level and your attention. All directed to one purpose: to become a better facilitator.

Land ahoy, Captain! Hold steady, keep the wind in your sails and your eye on the compass.

Part 3:
Sail into the sunset

To reach a port we must set sail. Sail, not tie at anchor. Sail, not drift… – Franklin D. Roosevelt

9. Prepare for success

How to get started with creating 'the moment'.

WHAT DOES SUCCESS MEAN? I consider my facilitation efforts a success when I managed to maintain a level of trust that allowed for all
participants to reconsider their old beliefs and achieve a new shared
comprehension of reality while becoming more and more committed to
act upon the purpose of the gathering. Preparation is everything, also in
'captaineering'.

Preparing for success. As a facilitative leader, you are preparing yourself
to connect your participants with their hands, heads and hearts.

Hands (Guide). People will be eager to participate if you can to make
clear to them what kind of output their work should produce, if you provide them with an appealing flow of steps, and when the pre-work was
meaningful.

Heads (Conduct). As you are preparing to connect them with their heads,
you are creating a situation where they are inspired by a diversity of perspectives, on online platforms or in offline spaces which are 'designed'
to support interaction, with sensible ground rules or agreed conventions.

Hearts (Catalyse). Your final goal is to get the group to act upon their
findings in order to walk the talk. In preparation to encourage commitment, you need a clear and inspiring purpose, avoiding pitfalls which
may cause doubt, with a shared understanding of what success of the
session looks like.

In part 2, I explained these elements of preparation for Guide, Conduct
and Catalyze separately. In this final chapter, the elements are reshuffled
into four easy steps to follow: framing, building, staging and owning.

You can find an overview of all 4 steps in Fig. 4 on page 171.

In this first step of your preparation, you define the purpose, the team and the output. In other words, the why, who and what. This is the basic information you need to complete the next steps of building, staging and owning.

Only when the why is well-formulated does it make sense to proceed.

Why. As I explained in Chapter 8, the purpose is the reason for creating a moment with the invited people. It is a crucial tool to drive commitment. Whether you are building the session on your own initiative, or you are being briefed by a sponsor or project owner, the first task is to articulate and agree upon the purpose. Only when it is well-formulated – and all involved parties feel comfortable – does it make sense to proceed.

Who. The next step to frame your session, is about determining who should be in this team to take on the purpose. It is a conversation about diversity and about quantity. It is also about buy-in and who will take the output further to an outcome. The team needs to have the right number of perspectives, decision power and capabilities to build on the output.

What. The final framing exercise consists of describing the kind of output. Is it a future service scenario, an agreed approach to move forward, a plan of action for all involved or a summarized consensus?
The expectations of what comes out of the session should be completely aligned before the session. The outcome is the result of work done on the output of the session. It also makes sense to determine whether this outcome eventually feeds into an impact, probably coming from a larger or longer term workstream. Distinction between the output, outcome and impact helps to align expectations, and it will avoid discussion about the results.

The **why, who** and **what** are also the perfect foundation for the invitation to be sent to all participants. For an invitee, reading and responding to the invitation is already part of the pre-work Therefore, it needs to generate excitement and eagerness to participate. A participant will easily become excited about the session if they understand what they will be contributing to, why their contribution is important, with whom they will synergise, and finally: what the format of their end result will be.

Framing the session creates clarity for you as a facilitator. This kind of clarity can help provide the confidence to build and facilitate the session, or series of sessions. When you understand context, gaps, goals, stakes, desired impact, strategy, you can decide on the readiness to move to the next step of preparation: building the session.

STEP 2: BUILD YOUR SESSION

When 'ready', the facilitator can start creating the session. Based on the context, and all available material, the necessary input for the session can be outlined. The input can include pre-work or homework, or it can be inspiration to kick off the session. The input is a determining factor for the different steps of the narrative. Once the input is clear, it is a matter of coming up with activities and topics which guide the thought processes to the desired output. The input and the narrative will drive participation. This when you prepare the structure of the session. The best sessions are built with empathy for the participants. To empathize, you might need to connect upfront with some participants to understand their perspective on the workshop. It is also a good idea to dig into the background and expertise of all participants. Some key questions to ask yourself as a facilitator:

- How can we build on what has been done before?
- Who from this team was part of previous work? Check with them.
- What kind of work and thinking are these people used to? What can I ask from them during the session?
- How well do they know each other?
- How will they experience progress during the session?
- What kind of 'closure' will they be looking for? (a detailed description, high-level agreements, etc.)
- Who from the team will be tasked to take the output forward?
- How comfortable are they with the purpose or challenge?
- What time of day are we having the session?
- What inspires them?
- What connects them?

As a guardian of space and purpose, and owner of time, their experience of the session is in your hands. When sketching out your narrative, I recommend you test it upfront with key stakeholders. Especially if you do not know the audience very well. It is better to do the extra work in advance than having to improvise and 'correct' your session on the spot. Your pre-work and narrative are important elements to build and maintain trust.

STEP 3: STAGE YOUR SESSION

Once the narrative is created, using inspiring and relevant input, it needs to be embedded into the 'space'. The first impression your participants get from the online or offline environment they arrive at will help kickstart the safe space. 'Staging' is about making sure everyone feels comfortable and excited arriving in this space. It will make them open up towards each other.

In an online environment, this means that you provide easy access and ensure everyone feels comfortable with making use of communication platforms or technology. Proactively thinking about potential technical glitches will save time when they occur.

In an offline environment, the space needs to fit the purpose of the session. If it is a creative session, for example, it is not conducive to have a U-shape or theater set up in a boardroom filled with furniture. You can also make us of the breaks and lunches to foster connection, conversation or creativity. Think about a lunch theme or break challenges or games.

When staging your session in an offline environment, also consider taking the group outside of their habitat. When people have been working in a specific environment for years, they have associations with the colors, smell and ambient experience of that environment. They might be programmed to feel stress when they enter this environment. If that is the case, it will take a lot more effort to maintain that safe space.

Owning means you grasp the session from all angles and perspectives.

Staging is just as important as building when it comes to creating the experience for the participants.

STEP 4: OWN YOUR SESSION

Now that the session has been clearly framed, well-built and staged for success, the next step is 'owning' your session. Owning means you grasp the session from all angles and perspectives.

Assess risks and pitfalls. After framing, building and staging, you will have enough knowledge about the participants, the goals, the input, the activities and the environment to start thinking about what could make this session difficult. What could happen that will disconnect people

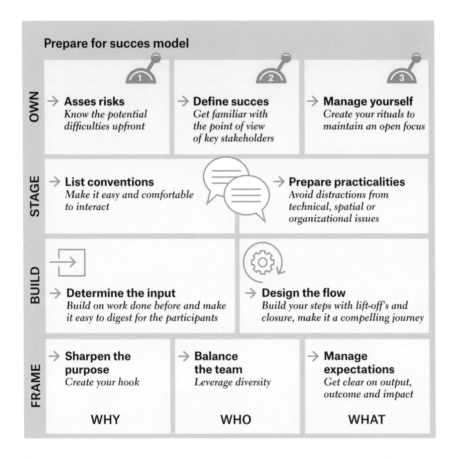

Fig. 4 A four-step model covering ten elements to prepare for successful Guiding, Conducting and Catalyzing. Providing structure as a guide needs a clear idea of output, input and a well-designed program. Driving engagement as a conductor requires a diverse team, agreed ways of interacting and well-organized practicalities. Increasing commitment as a catalyst requires a strong purpose, a good assessment of pitfalls and an understanding of different stakeholder's perspective on success. To prepare, first start framing the session. Framing provides all the necessary information for building the session. Based on the program, all conventions and practicalities can be arranged in order to stage the session. The final step is to assess all the risks, get a broader understanding of the meaning of success and apply your rituals for an open focus. In other words, owning the session. This four-step model is inspired by the 7P-model created by Dave Gray and explained in the book Gamestorming.

from participating, disengage them from deep conversation or decrease their feeling of ownership? For example, the internet drops out, the boss participates and dominates all conversations, no one prepared the crucial homework, the inspirational presenter is stuck in traffic, the large room was not reserved in time, a couple of participants have to step out for more important meetings or calls, etc.

When you own the session, you can still hold the space and lead your team to the best results, even if these things happen. It is because you have prepared different scenarios in your head beforehand. When assessing risks, you play out the session beforehand and try to come up with worst case scenarios, based on previous experiences or based upon the knowledge you gained while framing, building and staging.

Understand success. Influential stakeholders might have their own agendas or very specific ideas of what success looks like. It could be that they value the needs of the customer above all, or they have invested budget in another conflicting project. Owning your session means taking in account all the important stakes of key stakeholders in the goals of your session. You can have short informal conversations with key stakeholders beforehand to find out what their vision of success is.

Own your state. As part of your preparation, when the session is framed, built, staged and assessed, apply your rituals, habits and techniques to stay in a relaxed mindset. Managing your state is the final – and probably the most important – part of your preparation. Prepare for the unprepared. I have never facilitated any session that went exactly as I expected it to go. The beauty of facilitation is the adventure of the unknown. Every facilitation opportunity is a stepping-stone on your path of growth.

In the next chapter, I will explain how I build habits and rituals that help me manage my state as a facilitator. I hope to inspire you with some tips to stay balanced and confident during facilitation. Managing your confidence is about managing your emotions, your energy level and your attention. By creating your own rituals and healthy habits, you take control of your state. The next and final chapter is about sleeping, breathing and meditation.

10. Manage your state

Good captaineering includes taking good care of yourself. During all my years of facilitation, I have discovered three powerful methods help me to make sure I am rested, relaxed and sharp-minded. Here, I will share some knowledge, tips and tricks I have picked up over the years to help you take care of yourself with sleeping, breathing and meditation. It will help you to nurture your growth as a facilitator.

YOU CANNOT TAKE CARE of people if you do not take care of yourself. It is like the flight attendant will tell you during every flight: you need to put your oxygen mask on first. Because if you run out of oxygen yourself, you cannot help anyone else. When you decide to take on the role of facilitator, it is your responsibility to have an open focus. You need to be completely present in the moment that you have created for this group of people. Only then will you be able to bring the best out in the team.

Being the captain requires a sharp mind. You will be giving powerful instructions. You will be smoothly shifting gears on timing. You will be the first to see the blind spots or the potential of a shared perspective. You will direct attention by coming up with the smartest trigger questions in the heat of the moment. You will improvise when your prepared narrative turns out to be overwhelming or confusing. And you have the best understanding of the purpose of the session.

Besides having a sharp mind, being a captain also requires a high level of sensitivity. You will need to notice when people participate less, when they disengage or lack commitment to the cause and the team. You need to notice this before their irritation or stress levels will start to affect the others in the group. You will need to read personalities to be able to blend them together with orchestration and encouragements. You need to be aware of the effect of your own presence and communication style to maintain a high level of trust when reeling people back into the moment or getting conversations back on track.

KEEP GROWING

Of course, this is a description of the ideal situation. In reality, every gathering you facilitate is a learning opportunity. It is impossible to know upfront what will happen and how well you will facilitate. One day you are sharper and more sensitive than the next. The only thing you can do is prepare the session in the best way you can with the knowledge you have available, and to manage your state to increase your sharpness and sensitivity. Whatever happens in your session is an adventure. Every unforeseen event is an opportunity to grow.

Over the years, I have been facilitating workshops and meetings while I was in all kinds of states. I facilitated series of full-day workshops during two-week long conferences while having to attend social events until late in the evening. I have also facilitated while jetlagged. I have felt nervous and short of breath because of time pressure, high stakes and intimidating, high-placed attendees. There were meetings where I just was not able to explain anything properly, I just could not find the right words. All instructions were long-winded and confusing. And sometimes I was so nervous that I forgot to include certain activities in my program.

And even today, I end up in situations where I have a hard time driving coherence amongst the team. But with every learning opportunity, I grow as a facilitator. From experience I have learned that I can usually handle situations better – and have a steeper learning curve – when I make sure I get enough sleep and I control my stress levels by breathing correctly. Meditation has helped me to understand and manage an open focus.

SLEEP IS NOT A LUXURY, NOR IS IT LAZINESS, IT IS A NECESSITY!

Sleeping helps me to manage my emotions. We humans have been built to sleep for a long, continuous time during the night. In the ideal situation, we also have an afternoon nap. I used to think six hours of sleep was enough for me. But when I started sleeping between seven to nine hours, I woke up much more refreshed. I would not get irritated so easily and I was able to find my words more easily when presenting or taking part in discussions. It led me to investigate what happens during our sleep. Let me explain what I have learned so far.

Different people have different circadian rhythms. Your circadian rhythm is your internal 'sleeping clock' signaling when it is time for you to wake up or go to bed. Some people are early birds, while others are night owls. Teenagers, in general, have a rhythm of staying up late and waking up late. So yes, if you are a teenager and your parents complain about your sleeping in all morning, you can blame your circadian rhythm. But we all benefit from a sufficient amount of sleep. Sleep is like a reboot. When you are asleep, waste in your brain is drained with cerebrospinal fluid and your stress hormones are suppressed so that your body can recover from the day, especially from all those (d)emotions. In part 1, I labelled all the emotions which demotivate and deplete you of your energy as 'demotions', see page 47.

Lack of sleep has all kinds of unhealthy effects. In the long term it can cause – or at least contribute – to disease, and in the short term it will lower your cognitive capabilities. Obviously, this is very inconvenient if you need to bring your A-game as a facilitator.

When I first started facilitating, I would be preparing the sessions until late in the evening. Sometimes I would sleep for only five hours. But when I started to gain confidence as a facilitator, instead of rehearsing my facilitator role the night before, I would just briefly go over each step and go to bed early. Something magical happened. Somehow my brain continued to process the information during the night. The next day, I was much more on top of the session and all of its variables. Shorter nights, on the other hand, would often result in confusion and even overwhelm during facilitation. Ever since I have discovered the power of sleeping to process information, I always travel to the location of the session the day before, so I do not need to wake up early to travel on the day itself. This gives me a good long night's sleep, and I wake up refreshed.

Why sleep is refreshing. To understand sleep, it helps to simplify it a bit. We sleep in cycles that consist of several different stages. Typically, the cycle repeats itself four to six times during the night. It is not uniform: while one person has a sleep cycle of about 40 minutes, another may have a cycle as long as 100 minutes. For the purpose of this book, I will only go into the two commonly known stages of non-REM (or NREM) sleep and REM sleep.

REM stands for 'rapid eye movement', this is the sleep phase during which we dream. We relive and process the emotions of the day, but without any stress hormones.

NREM sleep is dreamless sleep, it does not include rapid eye movement. During NREM sleep typically there is less brain activity compared to REM sleep. During NREM sleep you are basically archiving your memories from short-term to long-term memory.

NREM sleeps improves your memory. NREM sleep is like reflecting on your day, storing new facts or new skills. If you would scan your brain for electrical activity during NREM sleep, you would see a kind of harmony. The thinking part of your brain (the cortex) is in a relaxed state and all information can be stored where it belongs.

When you do not get enough sleep, there can be a lack of refreshment in your short-term memory capacity and any new information from the day can simply be 'bounced' by your brain. Memories formed without the sufficient amount of sleep will be frail and they can easily vanish. The better your sleep, the better your memory works. When you are facilitating, your short-term memory and learning capabilities determine your sharpness in the moment.

Whenever I decided to stay up late the day before facilitating an intense session, it always had an impact on the quality of my facilitation. I had a hard time remembering names when I needed to call out someone, while using the right first names is such a powerful way to maintain focus amongst your team. During orchestration I would not be able to properly repeat what someone said, not to mention coming up with an unlocking trigger question at the right moment.

When I tried to MOH (Mirror, Open it up and Honour, see page 144), especially the mirroring part, I failed at replaying the contributions. I even chose the wrong moment to mirror, which made it sound less authentic and convincing. The worst part is yet to come. When I went to bed late, I would not be able to bring a crisp and clear 'big purpose – small purpose' whenever it was necessary. To me, reminding people frequently of why they are sharing the moment and why the specific activity is meaningful, is one of the most important tasks of the facilitator. It will keep everyone motivated and harness the energy in the room. My promise to be the guardian of space and purpose made me go to bed on time.

The better you sleep, the better your memory works.

REM sleep improves your creativity. The last stage of your sleep cycle is REM sleep. This part of your sleep is the facilitator's secret weapon. REM sleep, for one, has this amazing benefit of sparking creativity.

While NREM sleep stores new information, REM sleep starts working with this information, creating links between new and existing information stored in your brain. REM sleep brings us ingenuity. We might think that a daytime brainstorm will bring to the surface those completely new groundbreaking conclusions and solutions, but REM sleep is the absolute ruler of making unexpected associations in our brains. REM sleep is the reason why we sometimes wake up with a completely novel idea, which we just could not come up with while storming our brains the day before. It is so wonderfully simple and natural: a good night's sleep makes you more creative. The kind of creativity you need when building that compelling narrative, when creating that inviting safe space, when imagining all the different scenarios which could happen during your session.

When it is hard to find the right approach, it is a really good idea to just sleep on it.

When the goal or context of your session is complicated, when the various stakeholders have conflicting agendas, or when it is hard to find the right approach, it is a really good idea to just sleep on it.

REM sleep supports empathy. This might not come as a surprise. I am sure we have all experienced how hard it is to feel empathy for another person's feelings when you have had a short night. REM sleep helps you to regulate your own emotions better during the day. A lack of sleep can cause inappropriate emotional reactions, preventing us from seeing the bigger picture, seeing and considering other perspectives. The emotion centers of the brain become excessively reactive because of a lack of inhibitory control. In other words, lack of sleep makes you more susceptible to a narrow focus.

But REM sleep does not only stimulate our ability to control our emotions, it also helps us to interpret other people's emotions. This is a key element for facilitation and empathy. With enough REM sleep, you will be able to detect emotions from facial expressions much more accurately. With insufficient REM sleep, it can be harder to properly interpret other people's emotions. What is real and what you experience to be real are not the same thing. Without REM sleep, reading the social world around you becomes more difficult.

Imagine you are a bit sleep deprived, you are easily annoyed, it is harder to remember things, and when you need to improvise on the spot, your new ideas do not seem to pop up so easily. This is not the ideal state to Guide, Conduct or Catalyse a team into great output. Usually this rubs off easily on the participants causing them to disengage more easily. The same happens when you have sleep-deprived participants. The best advice you can give your participants is to have a good night's rest before your meeting or workshop. A sufficient amount of REM sleep will help them maintain an open focus.

LACK OF SLEEP? NO OWNERSHIP.

In my early days of facilitation, I was facilitating this workshop about improving the patient experience of kids during hospital treatment. One of the participants was not comfortable with the approach. She questioned almost every activity in an overly analytical way. I barely finished giving instructions and she would say things like 'I do not understand what you are asking us to do. In my opinion we should look at the data first and if we don't have the data there is no point in doing this exercise'.

Unfortunately, I had woken up early that day and had a short night. My morning felt rushed and I arrived a bit late. Her first comment, at the beginning of the session, made me feel irritated immediately. I needed a smooth start of the session. After her third comment, we ended up having a discussion and I expressed how I would appreciate for her just to trust the process and see how it would pan out instead of questioning it continuously. She did not agree with me. I did not know 'Bruce Lee' back then. Before I knew it, we had spent at least ten minutes discussing, just the two of us. I realized too late that the rest of the group was just waiting for us to finally agree and move on. They were disconnecting from our discussion and the session. Morale was low, and I only noticed this when people started asking for a break more frequently. After the break, almost all of them returned late. We finished the workshop with superficial conclusions and, as expected, there was little ownership to take anything further afterwards.

I blame my lack of sleep for getting worked up easily by the comments of the critical participant. I was judgmental about her right from the start. Everything she said confirmed my narrowed vision of her being on a mission to sabotage the session. I did not even see the effect it had on the other participants, how they must have felt. And on top of everything I completely forgot to break it open to the group when she gave her comments. Feeling empathy for her and for the group would have given me a much more open perspective and better approach to handle this. But Mr. Empathy was still asleep. I learned a valuable lesson that day, and I still think about it when someone openly criticizes the program in my session.

HAVE A SLEEP CHECK-IN

When you start your session, check in with all participants by asking whether they had a good night's sleep. Some might have been up since 5 or 6 AM for work. Other people have been working very late because of different time zones. Now that you know that lack of sleep affects your memory, learning capabilities, creativity and regulating emotions, your check-in will already provide a good view on the state of your participants.

Sleep well!

TIPS FOR THE BEST NIGHT'S SLEEP
— Sleep at least seven hours a night
— Avoid stressful situations right before bedtime, like watching your favourite thriller series on Netflix
— Stop working a couple of hours before bedtime
— Do not drink coffee after 2 PM
— Do not drink alcohol right before bedtime (rum is alcohol)
— Avoid waking up very early in the morning
— Reflect upon your day right before sleeping, focus especially on the things you would like to remember well
— Remember that lower temperatures induce sleep, so make sure your bedroom is not too warm

BREATHE DEEPLY

Breathing is the link between body and mind. And deep breathing is the most effective way to keep calm and focus. The way we breathe has a significant impact on our state, but also on our health. Shallow breathing is known to increase heart rate and blood pressure. Anxiety and stress can result in shallow breathing. And you might not be aware of it, but you probably do it all the time. Think about each time you breathe shallowly or even stop breathing for a second when leaning over your computer, dealing with your inbox and worrying about an

Controlled breathing is a perfect hack to control stress and strengthen focus.

upcoming meeting. Do you recognize this? It is called screen apnea. I learned about the benefits of correct breathing by doing yoga and meditation. And I have discovered that controlled breathing is a perfect hack to control stress and strengthen focus. Controlled breathing has helped me to become a better facilitator. Let me tell you how it works.

Breathe in through your nose. In his inspiring book *Breath*, James Nestor describes an experiment he did. First, he spent weeks only breathing through his mouth, followed by weeks of only breathing through his nose. (He actually taped his mouth shut to ensure he would not start to mouth breathe while asleep!) The experiment clearly shows how mouth breathing increases blood pressure and heart rate. It also affects the quality of sleep negatively, with all the consequences mentioned above. Nasal breathing, on the other hand, provides great benefits. I noticed the impact of nasal breathing by only breathing in through my nose and out through my mouth when I applied it during exercise. After some practice, I could actually run longer and faster.

Breathing correctly starts with breathing in through your nose. By breathing in filtered and warmed-up air through your sinuses, you increase oxygen uptake in your body. You engage your diaphragm more and take deeper breaths. This stimulates the lower part of your lungs which have parasympathetic nerve receptors. Thus, this type of breathing activates the parasympathetic nervous system, having a calming effect on the body and mind.

Breathe slowly through your nose. If you combine breathing through your nose with slowing the pace of your breath, the body enters homeostasis: a state of physical and emotional balance. The blood flow to your brain is increased and your body is in a coherent state. This means your heart, nervous system and circulation are syncronised into a state of high efficiency. Slow nasal breathing has a restorative and calming effect on body and mind.

Slow nasal breathing is an ideal way to get into the right state for deep listening.

Whenever I find myself in a situation that is causing feelings of anxiety or frustration, I practice slow nasal breathing. It is the easiest way to activate the parasympathetic nervous system, lowering my heart rate and my brainwaves to low beta or alpha frequency. This enables an open and creative state of mind. I breathe in and out without pausing, like the waves of the sea rolling in and out. Each inbreath and each outbreath lasts four to five seconds. It is a subtle way to direct your attention back into the moment, and the good thing is: you can practice it at any time during the day. No one will even notice.

PRACTISE:
SLOW NASAL BREATHING

Slow nasal breathing is an ideal way to get into the right state for deep listening, which is a very important aspect of leadership and co-creation. The next time you sit down with someone to carefully and empathically listen to their story, try to become conscious of your breath. Start breathing slowly through your nose, imagine you are lowering your heart rate. Take in the moment with every breath. Imagine opening your focus to every aspect of the other person. Try not to fill your mind with thoughts about your next question or with emotions you might feel in reaction to their story. As you breathe slowly, you hold space for them to fully express themselves. With every long outbreath, you sink into the shared moment a little more. You might notice how your open focus is stimulating the other person to open up as well. Your breathing is allowing a moment of deep connection.

Breathe slowly through your nose with extended exhalation. When during a session something causes a sudden strong surge of stress for some reason, I try to stay calm by using another breathing technique. I slowly extend my outbreath as far as I can, as if I were exhaling these feelings of stress. I extend my outbreath as far as I can without having to gasp for air when breathing back in. Inhaling happens slowly as well but not as extensively as breathing out. I breathe in for four seconds through the nose and out for six to seven seconds through the nose or mouth. When I repeat this for about ten breaths, it will reinstate a relaxed mind and an open focus. It induces alpha brainwaves and even theta brainwaves. Theta brainwaves are related to daydreaming and meditation.

In Chapter 6, I referred to 'blank space' as a way to disconnect for a moment during breaks. Practicing deep, extended breathing is a great way to create a blank space for yourself. Only focus on the breathing and let yourself slip into a state of daydreaming. It has a restorative effect on your body and improves your cognitive functions. Having this moment to yourself while you are surrounded by nature really is the icing on the cake. You do not have to sit down, you can practice this while slowly walking in nature alone.

Breathe for energy. While you can activate your parasympathetic nervous system with slow breathing for relaxation or focus, you can also do the opposite. You can activate your fight-or-flight response – your sympathetic nervous system – to generate energy. You might have seen professional athletes doing fast breathing to ramp up their energy level right before performing.

Sometimes when I have to give a keynote or when I have to start up a meeting and I don't feel it yet, I do a quick round of fast breathing. I breathe in and out through my nose for about ten to fifteen seconds, each breath taking about half a second. I envision filling myself up with good energy and generating elevated emotions like excitement and happiness. It is important that this feels like controlled, positive stress. As it activates the sympathetic nervous system, you need to make sure that you do not overdo it. Pay close attention to how your body responds and never force it. You know you have gone too far when you notice dizziness.

Breathing is an easy and natural way to manage your state. It takes absolutely no effort to experiment with and experience the benefits. It is also easy to teach anyone some easy breathing techniques to bring on focus and calmness. For the right audience, it is a great way to start a workshop or even a meeting. It can immediately calm everyone down and create a safe space.

TIPS FOR SLOW BREATHING
— Find a quiet spot to sit without any distractions. If possible, sit somewhere in a natural environment
— Keep your eyes open, but do not focus on anything
— Bring your attention to the breath
— Breathe in through your nose for five seconds
— Breathe out through your mouth with pursed lips, also for five seconds
— Extend each exhale by one second until you reach an exhalation of ten seconds
— You are now breathing in for five seconds and exhaling for ten seconds
— Repeat this for about ten breaths or for as long as it feels nice and comfortable
— End the practice by placing your hands on your heart and feeling grateful for this breathing moment you allowed for yourself

MEDITATION SUPPORTS FOCUSING YOUR ATTENTION

Enough REM sleep will help you to regulate your emotions and to avoid spikes in stress hormone levels. Slow breathing will get your body in balance and also decreases your stress levels. But what is it that causes the stress response in your body? It has to do with our thoughts. This, I discovered through meditation.

Two years ago, I challenged myself to meditating every day for 365 days in a row. I did a guided meditation every morning. They were between an hour and an hour and a half long. Up until then, I had only been meditating sporadically, and I felt I needed a structured approach to really experience and learn about the benefits of meditation. Also, I wanted to know if I could become a lot better at it and if I could have any mystical experiences.

In hindsight, these last two reasons were definitely not the best motivation for meditating every day. You cannot force meditation nor can you force having mystical experiences. Meditation is more about letting go and exploring the unknown than trying to master a technique. And this is exactly what I learned. During that year, I went through a rollercoaster of feelings and opinions about meditation. There were multiple moments of bliss and inner peace, feelings of oneness. But there were also moments of utter frustrations when I was trying to quiet my unsettled mind. The more I forced my mind to become quiet, the more it served up disturbing thoughts, often related to my biggest fears, for example thoughts about something happening to my kids in traffic.

I decided to quit meditation about five times that year, but I still ended up doing it every morning. Gradually I learned about acceptance and letting go. I finally began to understand what spiritual teacher Eckhart Tolle meant by 'Life isn't as serious as the mind makes it out to be'. After a few months of meditation, I could observe my thoughts without identifying with them. I was a lot less reactive to my thoughts, I just observed them and let them go. Slowly, thoughts started to appear less and less, and I was able to experience a kind of nothingness, which I believe is pure presence.

Becoming less reactive to my thoughts was a true blessing. It allowed me to manage perspective at any time, to maintain an open focus and easily generate empathy. Without tapping into passing thoughts – which could trigger all kinds of emotions – I will not let myself be distracted from the present moment. Being in the moment allows me to maintain an open focus. Let me explain this further.

Meditation creates more awareness. By taking time to sit down with myself in meditation and observe my thoughts in silence, I started to understand my programmed beliefs and how they trigger stress responses.
The first time I tried meditation, it was the most confusing and disappointing experience ever. I was in conflict with myself and continuously

wanted to escape from the silence. The more I tried to quiet my mind, the louder it became. My talkative mind brought up all kinds of thoughts which led to all kinds of (d)emotions. It was hard to even sit through ten minutes of silence with myself.

In Buddhism, this phenomenon of the talkative mind is referred to as the monkey mind. My thoughts jumped around like a monkey from tree to tree. And I was constantly distracted by these passing thoughts. These thoughts were about my to-do list, things I cannot forget, fears I struggled with, and so on. Each time a thought was able to trigger certain emotions, it became more intense and more distracting. And If I got frustrated, my brainwaves would get into a mid- to high-beta state, which is far away from the calm meditative Theta state. In other words, I was not meditating at all. I was just trying to sit still. It drove me nuts.

I did not stop trying to meditate. When I realized how active this monkey mind can be, I was determined to deal with it. And after a while, I understood I had to be the observer without trying to control my thoughts. By just observing the thoughts passing through my mind, I did not give them the attention that would fuel them with energy and stir up all kinds of emotions that reinforce these thoughts even more. They would not distract me as much by not judging them and allowing them to occur and fade away again. I became more aware of my thoughts and what it means to be present. And by understanding the distinction between presence and distraction, I could become present more easily each time.

Keep it up. Most people start practicing meditation but have a hard time following through. It is just like slow nasal breathing: if you stop practicing it, your former 'reactive' state will return. Your brain changes when you meditate, but when you stop practicing it, the old patterns of thinking, feeling and doing will find their way back into your habits. I believe the only way to really integrate these practices into your life, is to make it your own: find out what works for you. What time of day works best? How long is the perfect meditation for you? It does not have to be an hour, and it does not have to be early in the morning. It does not even have to be every day. As longs as you experience that it is working for you.

Find out what works for you and stick to it.

This is really is one of the key messages of this book: find out what works for you. It applies to all you have learned about facilitation, but also everything you might pick up from this part. The goal is to find what works and then turning it into new, lifelong habits. Adapt everything you learn into a practice that makes you feel comfortable. Make sure it does not conflict with time you need to spend on other tasks or with your family. Above all, it should never be an obligation or a task, it should be pleasurable.

During my year-long meditation challenge, I came to understand the experience of being the observer of my thoughts. I no longer tried to control them. This helped me to become less reactive, to regulate my emotions and to keep a calm mind. I became more aware of what it means to be present though meditation. These are no easy achievements. So, how did I do this? I decided to bring some measuring tools into my meditation practice.

The more I told myself to 'let go, be present', the more I seemed to force it and my brain remained active.

USING BRAINWAVE FEEDBACK

I started using two devices to help me on my road of discovery. The first one is called Muse. This simple app, which connects to a headset, provides real-time brainwave (EEG) feedback, helping me to understand what it feels like when my brain shows lower-frequency activity – like alpha cycles or even theta cycles. I activated the app during my guided meditation session. After each one, Muse would tell me how much time I spent in a calm state of mind. By matching the outcome with specific moments during the guided meditation, I could remember how I felt in that exact moment. The results were surprising.

There were sessions where I was certain that my mind was mostly calm, but the results showed otherwise. This happened especially when I was determined to calm my mind and tried to block passing thoughts. I had othersessions where I was certain that I did not achieve a calm mind, and then Muse would prove me wrong. At first it felt so contradictory – I was convinced that the device was malfunctioning!

But after while I started noticing patterns. When I woke up and allowed myself to start thinking about all kinds of things before meditation, I had a really hard time to quiet my mind. Sometimes, a very intense emotional movie or documentary – or conversation with friends from the night before – would pop up right after waking up. It unsettled my mind, and I had a hard time settling it back down.

The more I told myself to 'let go, Alwin, be present', the more I seemed to force it and my brain remained active. To deal with this unsettled mind, I started trying out breathing techniques instead of telling myself to let go. And this worked wonders. Applying conscious slow breathing had an impact on the EEG results. This made me realize how important breathing is to regulate your state. Not only did it help me at the start of the meditation, it also helped me to 'recover' to a calm mind during meditation.

MEASURING THE HEART

Beside the Muse app, I used a tool to measure heart rate variability (HRV) developed by the Heart Math Institute. This institute has been researching and developing stress reduction tools for over thirty years. Heart rate variability is the variability in the amount of time between two heartbeats. It is an indicator of nervous system balance and strength, and consequently your systemic health and resilience.

There are all kinds of HRV measuring tools on the market by popular brands like Polar or Elite. By looking at the changes in heart rhythm, I was able to measure the alignment between my heart, mind and emotions. A coherent heart rhythm synchronizes brain activity and it influences cognitive functions, like focus and memory. This principle supports the 'heart hug' technique described in Chapter 5. When I activated regenerative emotions like appreciation or compassion, it had an impact on my HRV results and brainwave feedback. I combined slow breathing with activating regenerative emotions focusing on my chest area, and it brought me into a calm meditative state more easily. When I apply the 'heart hug' technique, generating regenerative emotions, at the start of a session, just for a few minutes, I am more likely to maintain balance and avoid my sympathetic nervous system to easily be triggered. And this then results in improved cognitive functions, or a sharper mind.

A few months of practicing meditation and measuring HRV and brainwave feedback provided me with some very clear insights into the impact that my emotions have on my state. Now, I clearly understood what a calm, meditative state of mind feels like, and I was aware of the role that breathing and emotions play to achieve this state. Slow breathing, regenerative emotions and focusing on my heart area brought me into a calm meditative state much more easily. It became easier for me to maintain balance and activate the parasympathetic nervous system. And it improved my nervous system function in general.

Slow breathing, regenerative emotions and focusing on my heart area brought me into a calm meditative state much more easily.

START SMALL

If you want to create new habits, first find a practice that suits you. Then start small and practice frequently. Every time you practice meditation, even a short basic session, it will have a great effect on your body and mind. You activate your parasympathetic nervous system and give yourself a chance to restore. You do not need to become a master or an expert to experience this beneficial effect. Try not to put any pressure on yourself but enjoy exploring new ways of practicing these things. Expand your horizons and find out what works best in your life. There is no urgency, you have a lifetime of exploring ahead of you. But there is a difference between doing and not doing. Only thinking about it will not generate any effect or learnings.

The greatest motivation I can offer you is assuring that it does make you a better facilitator. Facilitation is about becoming more aware of yourself and others. It is about experiencing the shared moment more consciously. In order to do this well, it makes sense to have routines that train you to 'manage your attention'. For me, meditation has become a daily practice to do just that. It has helped me to grow as a facilitator.

An entry point to meditation. I will share a very short meditation that I practice every day. It helps me to be in the present moment with gratitude and compassion. It is like a work-out, teaching my mind and body to 'know' this state, so I can invoke it more easily during facilitation.

REBOOT

Intense events in our lives tend to leave their residues in our bodies and minds. Spending time with people in the moment, empathizing deeply

PRACTICE: HEART MEDITATION

1. Find a quiet spot where you are not distracted by anything or anyone. Play some soothing instrumental music if this helps you to block any distracting sounds. Make yourself comfortable sitting in a chair or on the ground or lay down. Close your eyes. If you are bothered by the light shining through your eyelids, wear an eye mask.
2. Slow down your breathing: slow inhales through your nose and slow exhales through your mouth or nose.
3. With each inhale, breathe in a feeling of gratitude into your heart, gratefulness to be here and to be alive.
4. As you are breathing gratitude into your heart, imagine a sphere, like a balloon, originating from your heart, and growing with every inhale. The sphere grows from the centre of your heart until it completely encloses you. You are now sitting and breathing within your heart sphere. It is filled with gratitude.
5. Every inhale fills this sphere with gratitude to be alive, every exhale blows any other thoughts gently outside the sphere where they vaporise into nothingness.
6. Keep inhaling gratitude into your heart sphere and exhaling any other thoughts into nothingness.
7. When you feel a strong sense of gratefulness, expand the sphere as far as you can while exhaling.
8. Inhale gratefulness and exhale a feeling of compassion for everyone the sphere can include. Exhale the sphere to such a size that it covers as much space as it can, including everyone and everything that lives.
9. Expand your gratefulness to be alive with compassion for everything that lives. Feel the sphere coming from your heart and expanding across the entire earth with your slow exhale.
10. Continue inhaling gratefulness to be alive, and exhaling compassion for all living things until you feel a sense of togetherness and oneness.
11. Keep breathing in and out slowly and enjoy this feeling of oneness for as long as you can or want.
12. End the meditation by putting both hands on your heart and feeling grateful for all the kindness you have recently received from others.

Do not skip the last step, it is the most important step of all. By acknowledging and appreciating kindness anyone has shown you, without asking anything in return, you remind yourself that this is a world of giving, not taking. It nurtures the right mindset to be a facilitative leader: a mindset of giving.

with them, and staying sharp and sensitive to Guide, Conduct and Catalyse, can leave an imprint as well. After I have facilitated an intense workshop, it often feels like I am still carrying a lot of impressions and emotions from that event. I need to recover from it.

A clear signal for me is when I dream about the workshop. I know it had a big impact on me because I need my REM sleep to process all of the emotions I experienced. When that happens, I know I need to reboot all systems. I have developed a personal ritual that helps me to let go, find closure and move on.

For this reboot ritual I free up a couple of hours of me-time. This ritual has three goals: it helps me to relieve myself of any remaining worries or stress, it is a physical 'reset', and it helps me to regain my sense of balance. You might already have your own ritual, or maybe you 'reboot' in different ways, I just hope sharing my ritual might help you to build or finetune your own.

Clear my mind. Exercise is a great way to distract yourself and break out of a cycle of thinking. The endorphins that are released are a welcome side effect providing a rewarding feeling of well-being. My ritual starts with a run: it helps me to put everything in perspective and deal with unresolved issues or feelings which might be leftovers from the workshop. As with meditation, I only observe thoughts passing by and I breathe in through my nose. Nasal breathing will force me to breathe more slowly, increase carbon dioxide levels in my blood and thus increase oxygen uptake in my muscles. This helps me to achieve physical balance during my run. It also forces me to breathe deeply, using my diaphragm instead of breathing shallowly at the top of my lungs. Because of the slower nasal breathing, I do not necessarily have to run that long to get the 'balanced' effect I am looking for. A short half-hour run with the right breathing can already do the trick.

Clear my body. After the exercise, I continue with a breathing technique that reboots my system. I practice the Wim Hof Method. It is a fast-breathing technique that activates the sympathetic nervous system in a controlled way and alkalizes the blood.

The Wim Hof Method consists of a couple of rounds of fast breathing. Breathing in from belly to head and breathing out in one continuous flow. You end each round by holding your breath after you exhale. Each time you try to hold your breath a bit longer, but it still needs to feel comfortable. After each 'breath hold', you breathe in and hold again for about ten seconds. Wim Hof provides multiple tutorials and guided breathing exercises in his typical no-nonsense style. If you would like to learn more about the Wim Hof Method, you can find all the information and courses here: www.wimhofmethod.com.

This fast-breathing technique provides all kinds of benefits, like stress reduction, decreased inflammation, increased clarity, increased creativity, better sleep, etc. But as with any new technique you learn, you need to make sure you understand it well first, and never force your body beyond its limits. This is especially the case with Wim Hof's method, which is derived from the tummo – or inner fire – breathing technique practiced in Buddhism.

In my ritual, this type of breathing exercise feels like a complete reset. The fast breathing brings my body into a controlled state of stress. Afterwards, I take a moment to lie down, close my eyes and induce a fully relaxed state. For better running results, you could also practice the breathing before the run. But in this case, my goal is not to achieve a better performance, but rather to achieve body-mind balance.

Connect to the source. The final step of my ritual consists of a short heart meditation session, as I described in the previous section. I consider the heart to be the source of creativity and also the connection to everyone and everything. The heart meditation helps me to complete the reboot ritual with elevated emotions of gratitude and compassion towards all people I connected with during the gathering. It allows for an open focus towards the project, which often generates new insights and ideas, during and after the meditation. Or even the morning after.

Cleansing closure. After the meditation, I have a cold shower and visualize a complete cleansing of body and mind, removing any residues of stress or negative emotions. If you are not used to cold showers, you can start with warm water and gradually lower the temperature. 16 °C is cold enough to get the benefits from the cold. You can train yourself by extending the time. Two to three minutes of cold showering should be sufficient. Make sure you continue to breathe deeply and slowly. This will help you to stay warm during and after the shower. You will notice that if you start breathing fast and short in the top part of your lungs, you will have a harder time staying warm, especially after the shower.
There are so many benefits associated with cold showers like better skin and hair, relief of depression, muscle recovery, circulation, immune system, fertility, but most of all it helps with a good night's sleep. Knowing the benefits of sleep, for me this is the most important reason to take that cold shower.

All the steps I have described promote restorative sleep: the physical exercise, the breathing exercise, the meditation and the cold shower. During NREM and REM sleep stages, all the information and emotions of the workshop will be stored an processed, so when I wake up in the morning, I am good to go.

After having shared my reboot ritual with you, I would like to invite you to develop – or expand – your own. It may contain elements like controlled breathing, running and meditation. But maybe there are other things that you know work for you: yoga, tai chi, walking in nature, a massage, swimming or kickboxing. If it feels pleasurable to you, play around with it and incorporate it into your personal ritual.

Restorative sleep, breathing right and meditation are ways to maintain balance in your body and mind and enhance your cognitive abilities.

RESTORE: THE POWER OF PLANTS

So far, I have mainly mentioned techniques and practices. But there is one more topic that deserves a place in this part of the book: plant medicine. This has really helped me to become a better facilitator, and that is why I would like to share some of my experiences with you. I realize this is a very broad topic, and I do not want to pretend to be an expert. All I know, the few practical insights I have, I learned from my beloved wife. She inspires me every day with new amazing facts about the power of plants. One of her inspirers is Adriana Ayales, founder of Anima Mundi Herbals, who has a tremendous expertise in plants and healing. Her range of adaptogens has a fixed spot in our kitchen.

A new way of thinking about healing and medicine is emerging globally. And plant medicine is a big part of it. While writing this chapter, I was in doubt whether I should include a part on plant medicine. In the end, I decided to include it, because it has really helped me to manage my state.

Consider this part as an addendum, just to get your attention to the possibility of using plants as part of your 'managing your state' toolkit. Let me tell you what has worked for me. I would like to particularly share some insights on adaptogens.

Over the last decades, and maybe even longer, we seem to have forgotten to breathe well, to sleep well and to be mindfully present in the moment. And we also seem to have forgotten about old medicinal wisdom. But times are changing. A lot of scientific research is being done on the benefits of adaptogens, and they have become widely available for anyone to investigate and purchase.

What are adaptogens? Adaptogens are plants and fungi that have the unique capability of correcting imbalances in our bodies, caused by our way of living. They have a specific intelligence, as they match what your body needs. This means that adaptogenic plants can have a different effect on different people. They deal with the negative effects of stress on our body, they have a restorative effect, and they improve our overall feeling of well-being. They have been used for centuries in ancient cultures. Both in Chinese traditional medicine and ayurveda (the ancient Hindu system of medicine), herbal remedies have been used for healing and rejuvenation throughout history. Herbs like ashwagandha, licorice, tulsi, holy basil, mucuna, rhodiola, and so many more, have been used for thousands of years in ancient healing practices.

How do I adaptogens in my daily life? This book was completely written on a magic potion of pure cacao, supplemented with mucuna powder, from mucuna beans, and reishi powder. Reishi is an ancient medicinal mushroom. I mix the ingredients with oat milk and warm it up to a maximum of approximately 70 °C.

Raw *cacao* as a healing plant was first used by the Maya civilization in Central America.

Mayans called it 'the food of the gods'. It is very rich in benefits. For one, pure cacao increases energy and focus because it contains theobromine. But it also plays a role in the production of serotonin, dopamine and anandamide, which enhances mood and aids lateral thinking. Anandamide has gained a lot of interest lately. It is a neurotransmitter that binds to cannabinoid receptors in the brain and body, stimulating a sense of happiness and mental wellness. Anandamide plays a large role in our overall mood. It also plays a role in memory, appetite, sleep, and pain relief. Low levels of anandamide have been linked to depression and anxiety. High levels of anandamide can be found in apples and blackberries.

Besides containing anandamide, raw cacao is also rich in minerals like magnesium, and it contains L-tryptophan, an amino acid that – among other things – supports healthy sleep. So it is also great as an evening drink.

Mucuna is commonly known as a brain enhancer because it contains L-dopa (or levodopa). L-dopa is used by the brain to produce dopamine. Dopamine is a feel-good hormone that assists with transferring information from neuron to neuron. Mucuna's dopamine-boosting action helps with motivation and it lowers stress levels.

Reishi is known to 'nourish the spirit': it creates a state of calm focus, relaxing the nervous system and the mind. It helps to relieve the stress of our daily lives. Reishi also decreases fatigue.

Before meditation, I drink a tea infused with *blue lotus* flowers. These flowers have been revered throughout history for their relaxant and aphrodisiac qualities. The plant originates from Egypt, where it was used to reach altered states of consciousness. The effects of blue lotus can be euphoria, it calms the nervous systems and induces a meditative state. It also improves liver function, strengthens the immune system, reduces stress, deepens sleep and lowers cholesterol. Blue lotus tea is the perfect tea to drink before meditation, but also in the evening before going to bed. It is yet another plant that induces deep restorative sleep.

Another way to promote a good night's sleep is to make a mixture of *ashwagandha* with oat milk and a bit of cinnamon. Ashwagandha is known to improve the quality of sleep because of the compound triethylene glycol, which induces sleep. Ashwagandha also reduces the effects and symptoms of stress and helps to lower blood sugar levels. Above all that, it stimulates brain function and memory.

This is just the tip of the iceberg of what plant power can do for you. But please note that if you are interested in experimenting with adaptogens, make sure you are well-informed of the side effects. Never take any of these plant-based medicines without knowing for sure there are no contra-indications for you. If you are not sure, please consult a nutritionist, an orthomolecular therapist or another specialist.

And thus, with this short section on adaptogens, the toolkit is complete. Of course, it is never really complete, but I hope that these rituals and habits which help you to manage your state as a facilitator, and as a person. I hope that they will be useful to you, or at least that they will inspire you to start exploring and developing your own rituals and habits for sharpness, sensitivity, calmness, focus and energy.

Now you know how to build your facilitative confidence. In Part 1 I explained that your facilitation efforts are valuable, moreover, they are a pure form of leadership. Your effort to achieve coherence in co-creation, every single time, helps to build a collaborative culture and uplifts interactions in an organizational system to benefit all stakeholders.

In Part 2, I introduced you to the holy trinity of facilitation, Guiding, Conducting and Catalysing, and provided concrete practices to build and maintain a safe space. These practices help you to build and maintain trust, direct attention and energy and create ownership amongst the participants of your session. I took these practices from my own experience so that you can experiment and shape them according to your own style and preference.

The final confidence boost, in the chapters of Part 3, provides you with a simple four-step approach to prepare for your success. It also provides you with some inspiration to manage your state and build your own rituals and healthy habits. Feel free to experiment, and do not forget to make notes in your captain's log.

Now, I would like to address you as a fellow captain and wish you a marvelous journey on your quest for captaineering.

Would you like te learn more? Go to www.captainsofleadership.com for information on classes and workshops.

Captain-to-captain

If you want to build a ship, don't drum up the men to gather wood, divide the work and give orders. Instead, teach them to yearn for the vast and endless sea… – Antoine de Saint-Exupéry

CAPTAIN OF LEADERSHIP, are you seeking to have an impact on the world, but are you not completely sure where to start? Or you are waiting for the right opportunity? Let me suggest facilitative leadership: it might be exactly what you are looking for.

Every big idea starts small. Cars, personal computers, penicillin, blockchain, … they all started out as a thought and then became something through experimentation, collaboration and partnerships. At one point, there was this moment when someone asked the question 'What if …?'. A moment when someone's idea became a vision that inspired a group of people to take ownership and create a new reality. The power of the moment that people share is generated by what you can make of that moment for them. A moment should never be just a moment: it can be a moment of coherence, of synchronized brains, of shared empathy, of worldviews colliding and bursting into new exciting possibilities, a moment when you have the opportunity to facilitate for the best output, outcome and impact.

Wherever you work or live, there is an unlimited supply of these moments. And they all have a potential for impact. All those moments need is trust, new perspectives and ownership. All those moments need is you, my fellow captain.

I hope that this book will help you to build your facilitative confidence. I see a world of captains who are on a mission to generate coherence between different perspectives in collaboration. A form of decentralized leadership which infuses our co-creation with empathy. If you feel more confident to take on this role whenever a 'moment' presents itself, I have succeeded as a writer.

To aim for your ownership of the captain's hat, I have stayed true to my own while writing this book. I was writing for 'lift-off' in part 1, explaining how facilitation is a pure form of leadership for anyone to take on when it matters. In part 2, I played around with pace. Some parts were short and others needed more color and description. Chapter 7 is the longest chapter, because 'Conducting' is really at the core of facilitation. It makes all the difference in the output. So, I made this a longer chapter hoping that you would spend a bit more time digesting the information and reflecting on how to apply it. In chapter 8, the focus was more on preparation to actually start doing facilitation. And so, we moved into Chapter 9 in Part 3, that provided four simple steps to prepare you for success, building on the learnings from the previous chapters in part 2. And then we slowed down to find closure by examining how you can manage your state as a facilitator in chapter 10. In this final chapter I want to emphasize that good facilitation does not come from applying the Guiding, Conducting and Catalysing principles exactly how I described it. Good facilitation comes from your sharpness and sensitivity, which is a natural consequence of the state you are in. If you can maintain an open focus, open heart and maintain your energy level, you will be a good facilitator even if you don't Guide, Conduct or Catalyse in the way I have explained it. If you manage your state and take care of yourself, you will probably find better ways to Guide, Conduct and Catalyse than explained in this book.

If you manage your state and take care of yourself, you will probably find better ways to Guide, Conduct and Catalyse than explained in this book.

Facilitation is not a skill, it is not exclusive, it is not an art, it is not a function, it is a dedication to self-awareness and empathy, it is a celebration of the shared moment and being an ambassador of presence. There are no official grades or certifications that show your 'level' of facilitation, there is no framework to evaluate someone as a better or worse facilitator. Your growth as a facilitator is measured by the way people feel when you facilitate their moment. I do not believe in mastery of facilitation as I do not believe in mastery of being human. Your learning journey as a facilitator runs in parallel with your learning journey as a human being, as a person. It is a life-long learning journey, without an ultimate stage to reach. It is about the journey, not the end goal. When you are a captain, you live to be at sea, not to arrive at shore. You aim to bring the people safely to shore, but your adventurous heart is at sea, where anything is possible.

You are the potential, not the manifestation! So do not identify yourself with the results of your facilitation. Explore your potential at every opportunity and enjoy it. Your potential will manifest itself in all kinds of ways. Sometimes it will be glorious, and sometimes it will be a challenging learning experience. Either way, your potential remains unlimited, your manifestations are always temporary.

When you are a captain, you live to be at sea, not to arrive at shore.

This is a book for heroes. This is a book for you, if you are willing to step up and be the facilitative leader to help others to get the best out of their shared moment. Heroes do not strive to be awarded in the end. They act out of love for people and life.

If you just take care of yourself and manage your state, you can be the greatest gift to the world.

Thank you for reading *Captains of Leadership*, you are now officially a captain in my book.

When you believe in yourself, you believe in possibilities.
– Dr. Joe Dispenza

Glossary

Heart is a sea, language is the shore.
Whatever is in a sea hits the shore.
– Rumi

BECAUSE I DO NOT use them in the conventional way, some of the terms I have used in this book may need some extra explanation. You will find them below, along with some terms I coined especially for this book.

Brainwaves

Brainwaves – electrical activity in the brain – can be measured with an electroencephalogram (EEG), where small, metal discs (electrodes) are attached to the scalp. Brainwaves are produced by electrical pulses from interacting neurons. Brainwaves come in various frequencies, some are fast, some are slow. They are measured in hertz (cycles per second). Five different bands of frequencies have been identified, and they all represent a different state of mind: gamma (32 - 100 Hz), beta (13 - 32 Hz), alpha (8 - 13 Hz), theta (4 - 8 Hz) and delta (0.5 - 4 Hz). All frequencies can be present simultaneously, but the dominant frequency shows the state you are in:

Gamma: heightened perception, expanded consciousness, peak focus, insights
Beta: high beta = stress, mid beta = answering questions, analysing, low beta = reading a book. Beta is the general state of consciousness during the day
Alpha = relaxation, creative state, visualisation, self-introspective, light daydreaming
Theta = daydreaming, meditative state, hypnosis
Delta = deep sleep, loss of body awareness, repair

Bruce Lee

In martial arts, when someone runs at you at full speed, you can use that momentum to initiate a throw. The force of the opponent is used, not blocked. You take control of the energy to let it flow in the direction you want. Similarly, when a participant 'attacks' by expressing their opinion in a dominant or overly critical way, you can be thrown off-balance as a facilitator. You feel the need to block or even counterattack. But the best results come from using the force: acknowledging the input, empathising with that person and building on that input to best suit the group and the goal of the session. Blocking only makes that person manifest their opinion even stronger. But when they feel acknowledged and understood, they will start trusting and following you.

Bruce Lee will forever be the greatest icon of martial arts. I have labelled this facilitator's technique in his honour.

Captain & captaineering

A captain is the highest-ranking soldier in the field. It is the person in charge of a ship or an aircraft. A captain leads while being part of the team. In this book, the captain is the person that applies facilitative leadership to get the most out of the team. I call the act of applying this form of leadership 'captaineering'. With the title of captain and calling the act captaineering, my intention is to elevate facilitation to a new status. You earn the status of captain if you are willing to selflessly lead a team to the best possible output.

Catalyst

In chemistry, a catalyst is any substance that increases the rate of a reaction without being consumed itself. I use the term metaphorically, to refer to all the actions you can take as a facilitator to generate commitment and ownership amongst your participants of the session. By catalysing, increasing a sense of belonging and significance, you influence the rate of interactions and initiatives in a group of people.

Check-in & check-out

A 'check-in' is a moment when you connect people by having them share their thoughts on a certain question, for example 'What would you like to achieve today?' A 'check-out' is a similar moment of connection, but at the end of a session, for example 'What is your most significant take-away from today's session?'

Both check-in and check-out are rituals to help people settle into the shared moment and close the shared moment.

Circadian rhythm

Your circadian rhythm is your sleep-wake cycle, which repeats itself every 24 hours. The circadian rhythms is synchronized with an internal 'master clock' found in the suprachiasmatic nucleus (SCN), which is part of the hypothalamus in the brain. The SCN reacts to light to direct the sleep-wake cycle. At the end of the day, when the sun disappears and it becomes dark, the SCN stimulates the release of a hormone called melatonin. Melatonin is released by the pineal gland in the brain and facilitates the transition from a waking state to sleep.

Closure

The act of closing an activity, a session, a conversation, a purposefully shared moment. Closure is a comfortable feeling about concluding something that led to a satisfying result or return. Closure, in this book, is an important ritual to help a team move on from one part of the programme to the next with a feeling of progress and enthusiasm. It regulates the energy level of the group.

Co-creation

Co-creation has the obvious meaning of creating something together. In this book, I use 'co-creation' in the broadest meaning of the word. In my opinion, people always co-create a new interpretation, conclusion, decision, direction, solution, ... when they spend time together with a clear intention.

If the time spent together does not have a clear intention, but the goal is to enjoy each other's company, I do not call it co-creation. Although some great ideas might accidentally come from a serendipitous encounter between people or a nice coffee chat. In this book, co-creation is the moment when people intentionally have conversations to agree or create something.

Coherence

I define facilitation as generating coherence between people. I do not use the word 'cohesion' because that refers more to sticking together as a team. With facilitation, you enable resonance between people's thoughts, having them listen deeply to each other and build on each other's perspectives.

Deep listening

Deep listening is also called 'generative listening' by MITx Professor Otto Scharmer in his book *Theory of U*. It is a form of listening with an 'open will', allowing for the new to emerge. Deep listening can happen when you have a calm mind and an open focus. It is a state in which you alternate between low beta brainwaves and alpha brainwaves, observing what the other person is saying without any judgement. This allows for new thoughts rising from your subconscious without expectations or without forcing it through analysis. It is a pure co-creative form of listening while holding the space for any new thoughts to arise but also to let go in order to keep the space open for new thoughts.

(D)emotions

I use this word to refer to negative emotions that demotivate us, which make you feel depleted. Emotions like fear, anger, frustration, anxiety, aggression, jealousy, resentment, guilt, and so on. These are the type of emotions that drain your energy and can trigger your sympathetic nervous system, your survival mode.

Divergent & convergent

Captains of the Leadership is written as a divergent book: it should provoke action and experimentation to create your own viewpoints and experiences related to Guide, Conduct and Catalyse. It is by no means a definitive guide to facilitation. The intention is to help you build your facilitative confidence by creating your own style and identity as a facilitator. I invite you to broaden the space, find other captains and inspire each other. A convergent book would have provided a fixed framework with models and definitions. Any of the definitions, labels, language, frameworks in this book are meant to be shaped further by your own experiences and interpretations.

Grouping

Grouping is a name for splitting a group of people into smaller groups or merging them into a bigger collective. Grouping means playing around with group sizes.

In-group

An in-group is a group of people who share the same interest, use the same language or terminology and share a similar identity. It is similar to the word in-crowd. When you are considered part of the in-group, you are seen as a part of the 'family', as a like-minded person, trusted because you see the world in a similar way.

Lift-off

I use 'lift-off' to explain the moment where you hhave fuelled the tanks with kerosene and created the velocity to have a group of people start working together to achieve something, to fly. It is that burst of enthusiasm and energy you spark to get people engaged into activity and interaction. It requires powerful instructions and meaningfulness.

Mirroring

Mirroring is based on the idea of mirror neurons. People and primates fire the same neurons when they do an action and see that same action. It invokes imitation and empathy. When I use it in this book, I refer to the phenomenon when participants start mimicking and behaving like the person they trust most. It could be the facilitator, but when a facilitator loses trust, it might be another participant. If you have a high-ranking person in the group, someone who has earned a lot of trust and respect, the participants may automatically agree and even start behaving like this person. Even when it is against the facilitator's recommendations or instructions.

MOH-ing

MOH refers to the three types of coaching when catalysing a group of people.

M – Mirror: this is not the type of mirroring I described in the previous lemma. Coaching with a mirror means that you replay the conversation that just took place to recognise the value of everyone's contribution.
O – Open it up: coaching by opening it up means that you have one of the participants acknowledge the other participants' contributions in the teamwork.
H – Honour: coaching by honouring someone's contribution is about hitting the pause button as a facilitator to briefly direct everyone's attention to a great contribution from a participant.

Open focus

Open focus is a low beta/alpha state of calmness and creativity where you remain open to all possibilities and see all the opportunities. It is a state that allows for empathy and deep connection. Open focus is related to the rest-and-digest state when the parasympathetic nervous system is activated.

Narrow focus is a high beta state of stress response when the sympathetic nervous system is activated. Your focus is more on survival and therefore you see the world from a more selfish perspective. This state does not promote empathy or creativity. People usually become very analytical in their thinking, in a state of narrow focus.

Pacing

Pacing is a word I use to explain the act of controlling the conversational pace. Sometimes the pace needs to slow down to encourage deep listening and taking the time to understand each other's point. But other times, the conversation has been circling and it needs to pick up the pace towards the conclusion. The team must cut to the chase.

Your tone of voice, the use of silence and the pace of speech can help to slow down or speed up the conversation.

Parasympathetic and sympathetic nervous system

The parasympathetic and sympathetic nervous systems are both part of the autonomous nervous system. The autonomous nervous system regulates processes in the body like blood pressure, respiratory rate, heart rate, digestion, sexual arousal, pupillary response, etc. These are all the systems that work automatically without your conscious effort.

The parasympathetic nervous system is responsible for relaxation, resting, restoring, feeding. It is also called the rest-and-digest system. When the parasympathetic nervous system is active, heart rate and respiratory rate are decreased, and the metabolism and immune responses are activated.

The sympathetic nervous system is responsible for the body's response to dangerous or stressful situations. Stress hormones like cortisol, adrenaline and nor-epinephrine boost the body's alertness; blood is sent to the muscles; heart and respiratory rate go up. It is called the stress response or fight-or-flight response.

There are ways to influence the parasympathetic and sympathetic nervous systems with breathing techniques, yoga and meditation. (Chapter 10, Part 3)

Pep-structions

Pep-structions are instructions given in a 'pep talk' way. The best way to give instructions is with some excitement in your voice, and to use easy and to-the-point explanations with a confidence that the team will handle it very well. Pep-structions will fuel the team with enthusiasm and eagerness to start collaborating.

Persona

A persona is a description representing a person, or a group of people, who share similar characteristics, like struggles, behaviour, opinions, etc. A persona represents a group of people that is the focus of the conversation or the problem-solving activities. They are the inspiration to come up with the desired output.

Purpose

When I refer to purpose in this book, I am referring to the crisp and clear reason why people should be motivated to spend their time and effort in the shared moment. I am not referring to the purpose in life, or a higher personal goal. It is important to understand that the purpose is the oil of the spinning wheels of the session, the fuel for doing the work, the reason for existence of the session. Therefore, it needs to be compelling and easy to understand, or it will lose the power to motivate people.

Separation

Separation is another word for competition. It is the opposite of oneness, of acting and thinking as a collective. It is the opposite of empathy and connection. Separation is acting out of personal goals despite of the greater good. A sense of separation goes along with a narrow focus. We alle live in this illusion. The higher your frequency of beta brainwaves, the more you see the world from that illusion. When you calm down and open up, it becomes easier to empathise and even get a sense of oneness. Acknowledging this illusion of separation is a big step for humanity. I believe elevating facilitation is part of this awakening. Becoming a facilitator contributes to this awakening. That is why it deserves a 'captain' status, a new interpretation of leadership.

Session, meeting, gathering, workshop

Facilitation is most popular in creative industries. It is often linked to workshops. In this book, everything you learn about Guiding, Conducting and Catalysing can be applied not just to workshops, but to any kind of shared moment. This is why I often use 'session' to refer to a shared moment. 'Workshop' and 'meeting' have a lot of associations already, so I have tried not to use them too often to avoid narrowing the relevance of facilitation. Whether it is a one-to-one, a larger meeting, a workshop or any type of gathering, it can always be facilitated.

Sofa syndrome

Sofa syndrome is what you get when you do the team's work for them, for example capturing thoughts by writing them or filling in tools. The team will 'lean back in the sofa' and throw thoughts at the facilitator to pick up on and write down for them. The participants feel less responsible and become comfortably dependent on the facilitator. It is important to always task participants to capture, connect or visualise their thoughts, and have them take responsibility to help each other to build on each other's ideas for better outcomes.

Spinning

'Spinning' is a metaphor inspired by the spinning wheel on your digital device when it is processing. It means you give your team a minute or a couple of minutes to reflect and let everything sink in. Silent reflection is such a powerful thing. It means calming your mind and allowing for new information to connect with what you already know or to trigger new thoughts and ideas. It is an 'Alpha' moment, and it can help to ask the team to practise slow nasal breathing and lower their brainwaves as they let all the new information sink in.

For more explanations,
visit www.captainsofleadership.com

Acknowledgements

This book has been written with the support, effort and love of some wonderful people:

Annelies – You add color to my life. You are the reason why I'm able to just jump when I have to. You are my moral compass and my beacon. All the beauty in my life exists because of you. This book exists because of you.

Magnus & Svante – You both give meaning to my life. Such energy, such light, such a great sense of humor, such wisdom and such kindness. You both inspire me every day, my little pirates!

Jos & Ida Put – Thank you for always being there for me, for always believing in me and for all the unconditional love.

Erik & Jochen Put – My brothers, so different from each other, but I recognize myself so clearly in both of you. All those moments we connected felt like coming home. Thank you for helping me understand myself better.

Maaike Mintjes – Dear Captain, your sharp eye and great understanding of facilitation has helped tremendously with getting this book in shape. I have enjoyed all our conversations. You have a great way of getting to the essence of things. Thank you for all your effort and support.

Gilleske Kreijns – This book would not have been 'readable' to anyone but myself, if it wasn't for you. The way you work your magic with words is amazing. I am so grateful to have been able to work with you. There are so many ways to write the same message, but there's only one way to make it enjoyable to read and you nailed it each time. Your efforts were instrumental, thank you so much.

Tine van Wel – From the first moment we met, I knew the book was going to look amazing. You are so talented and a joy to work with. The graphic design skills you brought to the table made everything come together.

Vincent Jorissen – I keep looking for reasons to work together because I enjoy our conversations so much. Your ability to empathize, your creativity and your project management skills are a real treat. Thank you for making this story come to life online.

Julie Harris – You are such a wonderful person with such an amazing energy, thank you for stepping in in such an enthusiastic and inspiring way to bring this book home. Even though you came in at the end of the journey, your advice and your insight had a huge impact.

Bionda Dias (and everyone at BIS Publishers) – Thank you for believing in me as a writer and as a storyteller. You took a chance with me, as this is my first book, and I am so grateful for it.

Arne Van Oosterom & Tim Schuurman – It's so great to have a connection with the both of you. Thank you for always making the time to have a wonderful chat, even though we don't have enough of them. You both planted the seed in my head of writing this book. Thank you.

And to all the amazing Captains I facilitate and deliver training with, Aster, Colette, Jeroen, Felipe, Valerie, Marjolein, Robert, Yuen Yen, … and all those numerous participants of the facilitation training so far, thank you so much for inspiring me each time, again and again. This book is written in honour of all of you.

We are all captains of leadership,
spread the word by sharing this book

Read by ... *(name)* _____

on ... *(date)* _____

Passed on to ... *(name)* _____

on ... *(date)* _____

Read by ... *(name)* _____

on ... *(date)* _____

Passed on to ... *(name)* _____

on ... *(date)* _____

Read by ... *(name)* _____

on ... *(date)* _____

Passed on to ... *(name)* _____

on ... *(date)* _____

Read by ... *(name)* _____

on ... *(date)* _____

Passed on to ... *(name)* _____

on ... *(date)* _____